A Titan Lite

Kaitie —
Thanks for being who you
are. So happy to have you
as my lifelong friend.
You are the glue that
keeps us all united!
You Rock! I love you
merry Christmas
Sheri

A Titan Life

*Live An Extraordinary Life
Through the Wisdom of Titans*

RUBEN LHASA

T

TITAN PUBLICATIONS

T

TITAN PUBLICATIONS

www.titanpublications.com

Titan Publications books may be purchased for educational, business, or sales promotional use. For more information, please email us at: contact@titanpublications.com

FIRST EDITION.

ISBN 978-0-578-67443-8

For my mother,
who taught me to be of service to others.

MAKE A TITAN DIFFERENCE!
10% of all author royalties are donated to help children
from low-income families from around the world
to achieve their dreams of a better life.

T
TITAN CONTENTS

T

TITAN PROLOGUE

"Nature yields her most profound secrets to those who are determined to uncover them."
— *Napoleon Hill*

I was living in my one-bedroom apartment in Los Angeles, California, when I received a phone call from my mother, informing me she had stage IV cancer. Shaken by the news, and being the only child in the family, I took the first plane back home.

It was during this time taking care of my mother that I, for the first time in my life, got in touch with my own mortality. I asked myself, ***"If I were in the last hour of my last day, what would be the things I would have liked to have achieved in my life for me to say, 'I lived an extraordinary life?'"*** From that moment on, I redesigned my life accordingly.

Since I couldn't afford any expensive mentorship programs on how to become successful, not only in business, but also in life, I went to the place where I could get access to all the best mentorship for free: the public library. After reading hundreds of biographies and books on mindset, mastery, business, science, health, fitness, spirituality, finances, personal relationships and happiness, and, by trial and error, I created a simple guide for me to live an extraordinary life according to my own value system.

Ever since, I've been able to turn my lifelong dreams into reality – still am: I went from renting a one-bedroom apartment in LA to owning different houses around the world. I married the love of my life. We have three beautiful sons. We get to travel all around the world, meet amazing people and live phenomenal experiences, but most importantly, I get to live the kind of life that I've designed for myself: My Titan Life.

Living an extraordinary life is simple. It's not easy, but it's simple. Its secrets have been around for hundreds of years and have been applied by Titans throughout history: Confucius, Hippocrates, Alexander the Great, Leonardo Da Vinci, Miguel de Cervantes, William Shakespeare, Benjamin Franklin, Thomas Jefferson, Ludwig van Beethoven, Charles Darwin, Abraham Lincoln, Ralph Waldo Emerson, Mark Twain, John D. Rockefeller, Thomas Alva Edison, Nikola Tesla, George Bernard Shaw, Theodore Roosevelt, the Wright Brothers, Pablo Picasso, Mahatma Gandhi, Winston Churchill, Albert Einstein, Ernest Hemingway, Jorge Luis Borges, Walt Disney, Mother Teresa, Albert Camus, Nelson Mandela, Jose Saramago, Maya Angelou, Martin Luther King Jr., Warren Buffet, Dalai Lama, George Lucas, Larry Ellison, Steven Spielberg, Paulo Coelho, Bruce Springsteen, Richard Branson, Oprah Winfrey, Steve Jobs, Bill Gates, Barack Obama, Jeff Bezos, JK Rowling, Elon Musk, the list goes on. This book curates said secrets for you.

Live a Titan Life!

Ruben Lhasa

T

TITAN INTRO

"Life is like a play: it's not the length,
but the excellence of the acting that matters."

– Seneca

Are you living or merely existing? I would like you to think about this question as if your whole life depended on it. Because your life does depend on it.

If you are not sure whether you are living or merely existing, let me ask you a few additional questions to help you clarify your thoughts:

1. Do you have a purpose in life, or **are you just wandering aimlessly through life?**

2. If you have a purpose in life, are you living it out, **or do you lack the discipline and willpower to get things done?**

3. Do you wake up inspired in the morning, or **is it hard for you to wake up in the morning?**

4. Do you find joy in your life, or **do you feel discontentment and frustration?**

5. Is your health in place, or **are you struggling with health issues?**

6. Do you have energy throughout the day, or **do you feel tired and fatigued most of the time?**

7. Do you know how to turn your mind into your ally, or **do you feel that your mind may be sabotaging your success?**

8. Do you go to bed a little wiser each day, or **do you spend more than an hour a day watching TV, surfing the internet, playing video games, checking your social media or gossiping?**
9. Do you have healthy relationships, or **do you stay in relationships that are toxic?**
10. Are you living a life of abundance, or **are you just looking to meet your immediate needs, such as paying your bills, keeping food on the table and having a roof over your head?**
11. Is your environment (country, city, house, office, people) conducive to your success, or **is your environment detrimental to your success?**
12. Are you contributing to making the world a better place, or **do you feel like your life is not leaving any footprints in this world?**

If you have answered yes to any of the questions in bold letters, then you're existing, but not fully living. If so, this book is for you!

You're Not Alone...

"To live is the rarest thing in the world.
Most people exist, that is all."
– Oscar Wilde

Most people in this world are merely existing. They feel that life happens to them, as though everything was outside of their control. They don't have a clearly defined purpose in life, and even if they do, they do nothing – or not enough – to achieve it! They stay in the same job for years despite being unfulfilled and unhappy. They live paycheck to paycheck, without ever obtaining any financial prosperity. They don't take any chances on improving their life, so they can maintain their current "comfortable" lifestyle. They have lost their enthusiasm for life, and do the same boring routine every day, even though they don't really like it. They stay in toxic relationships. The list goes on!

And then, we wonder why there are so many unhappy people, or why someone overreacted, or why the customer service we received at the store was so poor!

Titans, on the other hand, make the most out of life! They are in charge of their life. They have a clearly defined purpose. They wake up inspired in the morning. They have their health in place. They find joy in life. They grow into the best version of themselves. They have relationships that nurture them. They enjoy financial prosperity. They surround themselves with beauty. And, they leave the world better than they found it.

As Winston Churchill said, *"It's not enough to have lived. We should be determined to live for something."*

You Are Going To Die... Someday.

"Remembering that I'll be dead soon is the most important tool I've ever encountered to help me make the big choices in life. Because almost everything - all external expectations, all pride, all fear of embarrassment or failure - these things just fall away in the face of death, leaving only what is truly important. Remembering that you are going to die is the best way I know to avoid the trap of thinking you have something to lose. You are already naked. There is no reason not to follow your heart."

– Steve Jobs

Being in touch with your own mortality is one of the best things you can do to *live*.

Most people fear dying. They don't even want to think about it, let alone discuss it. There's an aura of fear about the topic, and it's certainly not something to be talked about in polite company. To do so will inevitably result in accusations about being morbid.

Instead of being afraid of dying, be afraid of not living!

Life is a gift; this is why it's called the present. Yet this present is given to us for a limited time only – we are born, grow up and die – and we often forget about the shortness of life unless we are reminded of its transience.

Some of us will wake up tomorrow morning, take a shower, have our coffee, say goodbye to our loved ones, and that will be the last day that our loved ones will ever see us. Some of us, the day after tomorrow, will go into our doctor's office to get the result of a routine check-up, and the doctor will say to us, "Sit down, I've got some bad news for you." And we'll be diagnosed with some kind of terminal illness. So how can you appreciate life more?

One of the best things you can do to start living is to walk through a cemetery regularly. I know what you're thinking 'that's gloomy!' Actually, it's not. It's one of the most enlightening things you can do for yourself! In fact, in many traditions, such as Sufism and Tibetan Buddhism, "death meditation" is a powerful practice.

Walking through a cemetery will inevitably stir some thoughts about your own mortality – what life means, whether you are living the life you are meant to be living and what's truly important in life.

Far from feeling morose, meandering among the tombstones and reading the epitaphs is strangely calming. Secluded within this haven of rest, the pressing "problems" of life (bills, work stress, arguments with your spouse, house repairs) become muted to stillness.

If you read the epitaphs, you will notice that some of the souls resting in the cemetery were born the same year you were born; others were only teenagers, while others were just children. How dare you complain about your life!

And that's the thing about cemeteries: rich or poor, powerful or powerless, famous or unknown, our lives come down in the end to a resting place in the earth. If we are at all aware, this proximity to death has an instant centering effect. Like a good meditation practice, walking through a cemetery focuses our attention on what really matters, helping us to differentiate between what is important and lasting from what is unimportant and transient.

Leaving the cemetery, you will thank the dead for returning to you the gift of life.

Minimize Your Regrets.

"A man is not old until regrets take the place of dreams."
– John Barrymore

Too often we go through life on autopilot, going through the motions and having each day pass like the one before it. That's fine until we have gone through another year without having done anything, or until we have reached old age and look back on life with regrets, or until we see our kids go off to college and realize that we missed their childhoods.

One key to living a Titan Life is *to minimize the number of regrets you will have at the end of your life.*

If you're reading this, know that you're an extremely lucky person because it means you are alive! And being alive brings you the opportunity to make the best out of your life, regardless of the time you have left.

Bronnie Ware, an Australian nurse who spent a long time working in palliative care, knows more than most of us about the thoughts, fears and doubts of the dying. According to Bronnie, the number one regret most of us have when we are near our death is: *I never pursued my dreams.*

Most of us go through life trying to meet other people's expectations and not living the way we actually wanted to. Most of us never even reflect on what we truly want out of life. We simply go on "autopilot": we go to school; we go to college; we start working; we get married; we have children; we settle for a job that's "secured" (by the way, there's nothing "secured" in life), so we can continue providing for our family; eventually, we retire; and then, we die.

If this is the existence you want, nothing is wrong with it! But if a small voice inside of you says, *"There must be a better way,"* then, by all means, find another way!

The owner of one of my favorite restaurants in Los Angeles, California, always wanted to move to Australia and pursue his passion for surfing. One day, he sold his restaurant to one of his employees and moved to Australia.

A year later, I went to the same restaurant, and found the former owner back at the restaurant, this time, working as a waiter for his former employee. It was bizarre for me to see this.

"How was Australia?" I asked the former restaurant owner.

"I didn't like it. It was not the way I expected it," he replied.

"Oh, I'm sorry…" I said, trying to console him.

"No, it's actually great because now I know that I don't want to be a surfer in Australia. I tried it. It was not for me…" he replied with a big smile on his face.

I found his reasoning simply brilliant. What he was actually saying was, *"Now I know that when I get older, I will not say to myself, 'I should've tried it, but never did'.*

As Dr. B.J. Miller, a hospice and palliative care specialist in San Francisco, says, *"Loss is one thing. Regret quite another."*

Follow Your Dreams!

"The biggest adventure you can ever take is to live the life of your dreams."
– Oprah Winfrey

If there is a single practice that will greatly improve your life is *to follow your dreams*. Here's why:

1. **It brings purpose to your life.** Dreams makes your life worth living.

2. **You become more confident.** People who chase their dreams are sure of themselves and their life goals – nothing stands between them and their dreams.

3. **You wake up inspired in the morning.** People who dream – and act upon their dreams! – feel energized from the moment they wake up.

4. **It gives you a reason to live.** Your dreams are what can get you through even the worst days. If you are struggling, your dreams are your reason to keep going.

5. **You will provide for your family greatly!** When you're motivated by your dreams, it's very hard to fail!

6. **You find new skills.** When you work on your dreams, you will discover latent skills hidden in plain sight.

7. **Your environment improves.** When you follow your dreams, you are far more likely to find like-minded people doing the same and help each other in unexpected ways.

8. **You become happier.** When you're busy working on your dreams, you no longer have the time or energy to spend it on people or things that do not contribute to your dreams (toxic people, videogames, alcohol, drugs, gossiping, watching TV, surfing the internet, watching porn.)

9. **It brightens your future while being in the present.** When you work on your dreams today, your future suddenly seems more positive and brighter. Making a small step toward your dreams every day will make your future look more optimistic.

10. **You will contribute to making the world a better place.** By working on your dreams – and achieving them, you show people possibility and inspire them to follow their own dreams.

'Am I too old to follow my dreams?' you might be wondering. Here's my answer: *You're never too old to follow your dreams.*

'I always wanted to be a football player, but I'm now in my forties," you may say. Here's my reply: *Become a football coach, become a football agent, found your own local football club.* The possibilities are endless. Get creative about finding different ways to follow your dreams!

'What if my dream gets shattered?' you may wonder. First, if you think this way, *know* that your dream will most likely get shattered. But here's my reply: *A shattered dream is far better than a shattered life. So go for your dreams!*

Ask yourself, what would you do if you were to die soon? What dreams would you follow? What are you passionate about? What small action could you take today to start working on your dreams? Follow your dreams before you get to the end of your life. Then, it may be too late.

As Fyodor Dostoyevsky said, *"The mystery of human existence lies not in just staying alive, but in finding something to live for."*

Know Thy Dreams.

*"Definiteness of purpose is the starting
point of all achievement."*
— *W. Clement Stone*

The first step toward following your dreams is to *know what your dreams are*. I know it sounds silly, but you'd be surprised to know that most people don't really know what they want out of life. This is why they are constantly sending mixed messages to the universe. Not surprisingly, they never achieve their dreams!

Titans know exactly what they want and make sure they send clear and direct messages to the universe. This is why they achieve their dreams!

So if you don't know your dreams, don't say you never had a chance to achieve them! This is a fine world for the person who knows exactly their dreams and is busy achieving them!

By now, you're probably thinking, *'Ok, great. I got it. I need to know my dreams. But how do I know what my dreams really are? Where do I get started?"*

The Deathbed Exercise.

"I wanted to project myself forward to age 80 and say, 'Okay, now I'm looking back on my life. I want to have minimized the number of regrets I have'."

– *Jeff Bezos*

The name of this exercise might not sound very appealing to you, but trust me, it's one of the most life-changing exercises you can do for yourself.

If you are like most people, you have never made the time to *visualize* the type of life you want to live. At times, you might have fantasized about living in a beautiful mansion, driving a Rolls-Royce or having your own private jet, but very few of you have actually taken the time to really visualize the type of life you want to live.

The *deathbed exercise,* which is all about envisioning your Titan Life, has been shown to boost people's positive emotions, happiness levels and optimism, improve coping skills and elevate positive expectations about the future. By doing this exercise, you will get to know yourself, *your real self.* You're the only person who can figure out what you want in your life.

Spend as much or as little time on it as you want. In my experience, you will need at least an hour. You're designing your entire life, so take your time!

Are you ready to design your life? Please follow these 10 steps:

1. **Take a notebook and a pen.** Yes, an "old" notebook and a pen! With your creativity, handwriting is much better than typing on your computer.

2. **Go to a quiet place by yourself.** It could be a park, a beach, a public library, your bedroom.

3. **Make sure all of your electronic devices are turned off,** so you will have no distractions.

4. **Mentally fast-forward your life to *the last hour of your last day*, i.e., your deathbed.** Visualize that moment. Where are you? Are you in a hospital room? At your home? Where's home? What can you see through the window? Is it the ocean, the mountains, the city skyline? Who are you with? Are you alone? Are you accompanied by your spouse? Your children? Grandchildren? (Even if you have not met some of these people yet, visualize their presence.)

5. **And here's the question to ask yourself**: *What are the dreams you will have to have achieved for you to say 'I lived an extraordinary life'?*

6. **Write those dreams on your notebook**, no matter how "crazy" they might seem. Do you want to travel the world? Write it down. Do you want to own an airline company? Write it down. Do you want to become a best-selling author? Write it down. Whatever you want to achieve, write it down on your notepad. Don't forget to consider all of the relevant areas of your life, such as your health, family, career, relationships, legacy, finances, hobbies. Take your time. The more specific you are, the more engaged you will be in the exercise and the more you'll get out of it.

7. **Go back to the present.** Your mission in life is *to close the gap between where you are today and where you want to be in the future.* And you close this gap simply by *taking action*!

BECOME THE TITAN OF YOUR LIFE!

Here are some Titan quotes you might enjoy:

"The evening of a well spent youth brings its lamps with it." – Joseph Joubert.

"The symphony of life should end with a grand finale of peace and serenity and material comfort and spiritual contentment." – Lin Yutang.

"Do not let the hero in your soul perish in lonely frustration of the life you deserved." – Ayn Rand.

T

TITAN PRINCIPLES

"Principles are like seeds; they are little things which do much good, if the mind that receives them has the right attitudes."
— *Seneca*

Regardless of your current station in life or circumstances, the following five Titan Principles will help you pour a solid foundation to build your Titan Life.

Move away from these principles and the likeness of succeeding will be fleeting. Embody these principles thoroughly – and let them guide and direct your every thought, emotion, decision, and behavior – and you'll be on your way to building true and lasting success in both your personal and your professional lives.

Here are the 5 Titan Principles:

1. Take 100% Responsibility Of Your Life.

"I am the master of my fate; I am the captain of my soul."
— *Nelson Mandela*

Whether you think life is beautiful or difficult, you are equally right. Life is neither beautiful nor difficult; it is neutral. Life in itself has no meaning. It is *us* who give meaning to life.

One of the most empowering – and frightening – things you have to realize is that *you get to live your life the way you choose.*

I encourage you to read the above sentence again because, unless you fully understand this, and engrave it in your brain, you will never enjoy a Titan Life.

You may be thinking, *'Well, I wish I could live my life the way I choose, but there are many things in my life that I can't control.'*

Even if certain events in your life are outside of your control, you may still control one thing, and that is your reaction to said events. Therefore, *you do get to live your life the way you choose.*

A big part of you might still fight this idea. And the reason you might still fight this idea is that if you get to live your life the way you choose, this would imply *accountability and responsibility*. This would mean you would have *to accept ownership for your actions and outcomes.* And most people don't like this! Most people don't want to accept that the type of life they enjoy, they are responsible for. It's so much easier to say, *"I have such bad luck"* or *"I got fired"* or *"If I had more money"* or *"If I had better connections".* After all, we are simply the best at rationalizing why we are in the bad situation we are in. But these are simply excuses to continue postponing the self-examination and decision-making necessary to create a Titan Life. And beneath every excuse, there's always fear.

While most people make excuses, Titans make things happen. While most people say, *"Life happens to me,"* Titans say, *"I make life happen."* While most people say, *"What if it doesn't work?"* or *"I hope it works,"* Titans say, *"It will work because I will make it work."*

Your current business and personal lives result from the choices *you* made in the past. No one else is responsible! If you want to have a better life in the future, you must take 100% responsibility for your life!

When tennis player Rafael Nadal was about 15 years old, he was playing a tournament. His uncle and coach, Toni Nadal, was watching another kid from his academy play. Nadal was losing badly. A friend of the family noticed that Nadal was playing with a broken racket, and he informed uncle Toni accordingly. Toni immediately went to the court where his nephew was playing to tell him he was playing with a broken racquet. And then, Toni asked his nephew, *"With all your experience, didn't you realize that you were playing with a broken racket?"* A 15-year old Nadal replied: *"I'm so used to taking responsibility for my own mistakes that it never crossed my mind that I was playing with a broken racquet."*

2. Leave The Herd!

"The object of life is not to be on the side of the majority, but to escape finding oneself in the ranks of the insane."
– Marcus Aurelius

You can fit in or you can change the world, but you can't do both.

If you do the things that 95% of the population does, you will get the results that 95% of the population gets. Therefore, *if you want to get the results that only 5% of the population gets, you must be willing to do the things that only 5% of the population is willing to do.*

Don't be part of the 95%! Don't do what's popular. The most popular restaurant in the world is McDonalds. The most popular drink, Coca-Cola. Are they good for you? We both know the answer.

Titans have the habit of doing the things that most people don't like doing. They don't necessarily like doing them either, but *their dislike is subordinated to their Titan goals.*

Live completely different from the way most people live. *To live a Titan Life, you must install the beliefs, behaviors, habits and rituals of Titans.* Having a Titan Life is simple; it's not easy, but it's very simple.

It's not easy because mediocrity calls you in. I would like to clarify that to me, the word 'mediocrity' does not refer to someone who does not have a mansion or does not drive a specific type of car. To me, 'mediocrity' refers to someone unhappy with his life and does nothing about it!

Whether or not you aim for rich (this is completely up to you!), *always aim for having a rich life!* You may be a surf instructor and have a Titan Life!

My family and I spend a big part of the year on an island in Thailand. To most Westerners' standards, this island would be considered a "poor place." But I have seen more poverty of the soul in many Western, so-called "rich" countries than on this island. Everyone smiles here, and to me, whether financially rich or poor, it is indicative they are living Titan Lives.

If you are committed to leaving the herd, be ready for its consequences. Because when you act like only 5% of the population does, the remaining 95% will call you "strange," "weird," and "eccentric." Get used to it because this is the price all Titans must pay!

People get threatened when you show them *possibility* – what they could also achieve. But as we saw in Principle #1, this would mean they would have to take full responsibility for their own lives. So it's much easier to criticize you.

One of the biggest ways we limit our potential and deny our own Titan is following the herd and modeling the crowd. You must break free of the cult of mediocrity. You must stop listening to the chattering voices of the cynics around you. And you absolutely must trust yourself – and your instincts. And that's what every Titan does.

3. Grow Yourself Into A Titan.

"Life is growth. You grow or you die."
– Phil Knight

Everything alive is constantly changing. Take any plant, for instance. If a plant is not growing, it is dying. Same with people: *if you are not growing, you are dying,* at least, spiritually.

Your outer world is merely a reflection of your inner world. *You are the root; your results are the fruits. To change the fruits, you will first have to change the roots.*

Some people say, "This is the way I am." Well, change it! Because it's not working for you or anyone around you!

No matter who you are or what your background is, *you can always change.* Be willing to let go of having to do it "your way." If your way has proved satisfactory in the past, then, by all means, keep doing what you are doing. But if not, it may be time to consider a different way!

There are two kinds of people in life: those who *evolve* and those who *devolve.* Even those who falsely believe in the "status quo" are actually devolving. How would you feel if ten years from now you would be exactly where you are now, with zero growth? You guessed it! Bitter, miserable and unhappy.

So the question is, *Who must you become to live your Titan Life?*

Becoming healthy, rich and happy isn't much about getting healthy, rich and happy. It's about *who you must become in mind, body, spirit, heart and skill* to get healthy, rich and happy.

So the fastest way to become a Titan is *to work on developing you.* If you grow yourself to become a Titan in strength of mind, body, spirit, heart and skill, you will naturally be a Titan in anything and everything you do.

If you look at Titans around the world, they think and act in very similar ways. And these ways of thinking and acting determine their Titan results.

Proper training of your spirit, mind, body, heart and skill is essential!

4. Take A Holistic Approach To Life.

"In fact, if I'm happy at work, I'm better at home – a better husband and better father. And if I'm happy at home, I come into work more energized – a better employee and a better colleague."

– Jeff Bezos

Thanks to epigenetics, we now know that nutrition, exercise, sleep, the environment, the books you read, your family relationships, the conversations you have, the words you speak, even the air you breathe all affect your DNA and the quality of your life!

Your spouse, your income, your happiness, the way you treat others all reflect your self-identity. If you want to live a Titan Life, *you must take a holistic approach to life.*

You may have all the money in the world, but if you have no one to share it with, it will be a hollow victory. Or you may be a very spiritual person, but if you can't pay your bills, this will, sooner or later, cause stress in your life – and those around you! Or you may exercise and eat organic foods, and you're still getting sick??

The key word is *harmony.* Rather than striving to achieve some false "constant balance" in your life, it's about arranging your life, so the different parts are in harmony. The key difference is that harmony means you can focus more on work sometimes and more on your family other times. *You don't always have to force everything to work at once.* Titans pay attention to this!

Whether you like it or not, *all the different aspects of your life are inextricably tied up together.* If you neglect one of them, it's not possible to live a Titan Life.

Titans are part warrior, part saint. They are confident, but humble. They are winners, but never lose their white-belt mentality. They are content, but never satisfied. They focus on success, but also on making a difference. They play golf at the country club, but also serve meals to the homeless. They love thinking and dreaming, but also executing on their ideas and dreams. They are delusional about how great they can be but realistic about their expectations of the process.

While most people must choose one or the other, Titans know that *you can have it all!* You must simply transition from a mentality of scarcity and limitation to one of possibility and abundance! Yes, it will take many sacrifices along the way. Yes, it won't be easy. But it's simple and so worth it!

5. Create Your "Titan Luck."

"I'm a great believer in luck. The harder I work, the more luck I have."

– *Thomas Jefferson*

There's a difference between luck and Titan Luck. Luck, you have no control over. It's random chance. It's a winning lottery ticket. Titan Luck, on the other hand, *you create it.* Titans believe in the latter, while most people believe in the former type of luck. This is why lottery tickets, all around the world, are many people's "only shot" at a better life. *If people only knew that they could create their own Titan Luck!*

Does luck, then, exist? Yes, it does. But since you can't control this type of luck, why focus on it? Why wait for this type of luck to happen randomly?

To most people, luck is important. To Titans, it's less important. While acknowledging the existence of luck, Titans do not rely on it to live a Titan Life.

Let's look at the life of Bill Gates to better illustrate the difference between luck and Titan Luck.

Bill Gates got lucky in the sense that:

- he was born into an upper-middle-class family with the resources to send him to a private school;

- his school had a Teletype class, which gave him access to a computer; and

- his friend Paul Allen showed him an article in *Popular Science* magazine about a new computer called the *Altair 8800.*

Bill Gates had no control over the above events. So we could say these were "lucky events." Now the question to be asked is: "Is *luck* the reason Bill Gates became a Titan?" Far from it! Here's why:

- he was not the only person who grew up in an upper-middle-class family.
- he was not the only one with access to a computer in the 1950s.
- he was not the only one who read the article in *Popular Science* magazine.

Thousands of people with the same lucky events could have done the same thing that Bill Gates later did, but they simply didn't. So what did Bill Gates do differently from thousands of people with the same initial lucky events?

- he had an incessant drive.
- he dropped out of college and moved to Albuquerque to work with Altair.
- he barely slept and ate, so he could work longer hours.
- he was fanatical about writing good software.
- he didn't believe in weekends or vacations.

Bill Gates *actively created the conditions* to bring himself Titan Luck. And this, you have control over!

Here are the five Titan Principles for your review:

1. Take 100% responsibility for your life.
2. Leave the herd!
3. Grow yourself into a Titan.
4. Take a holistic approach to life.
5. Create your "Titan luck."

T

TITAN VISION

*"The world turns aside to let any man pass
who knows where he is going."*

– *Epictetus*

A Titan Vision is a clearly defined vision of the type of life you want, so at the end of your life, you can say, *"I lived an extraordinary life."* Without a Titan Vision, you will never get there!

All Titans have a clear vision of their future:

- Arthur Guinness signed a lease for the St. James's Gate Brewery for 9,000 years.
- Eleanor Roosevelt had a vision of a world of equal opportunity for women and minorities.
- John F. Kennedy famously dreamed of putting a man on the moon.
- Nelson Mandela had a vision for the eradication of racism and for the establishment of a constitutional democracy in South Africa.
- Arnold Schwarzenegger had a vision of becoming bodybuilding champion and a Hollywood movie star.
- J.K. Rowling planned out the seven books of the Harry Potter series before she even wrote the first one.
- Roger Federer had a vision of becoming the best tennis player in the world.

These are just a few examples, but know that *there isn't a single Titan who became so without having a Titan Vision.*

Why A Titan Vision.

"Shall we not, like archers who have a mark to aim at, be more likely to hit upon what is right?"
— *Aristotle*

We humans need a clear target at which to aim. Otherwise, we are left with the "animal default." And since animals live in herds, we wander through life and conforming to the group's vision — or lack thereof —, which results in anguish, bitterness and a lack of enthusiasm for life. A Titan Vision acts as your "North Star," giving direction to your life.

Your Titan Vision is unique for you. Whether it is becoming a best-selling author, building a business that makes a difference, writing a song that touches people's lives, creating a non-profit you care about, fighting for social justice, raising a child that will become a great human being, traveling around the world so you can learn about what binds us as human beings, whatever it is, only you know what your Titan Vision is.

And once you have your Titan Vision clearly defined, *your feelings, thoughts, words, actions and habits will all align in service of your Titan Vision,* and your choices in life will be simplified — either they will contribute to your Titan Vision or they won't.

As Johann Wolfgang von Goethe said, *"Until one is committed, there is hesitancy, the chance to draw back. Concerning all acts of initiative (and creation), there is one elementary truth that ignorance of which kills countless*

ideas and splendid plans: that the moment one definitely commits oneself, then Providence moves too."
Make the time to think about what your Titan Vision in life is. *When it comes to your own life, be a leader. Otherwise, the herd will lead you.*

Have A Vision Larger Than Yourself.

"The greatest danger for most of us is not that our aim is too high and we miss it, but that it is too low and we reach it."
– Michelangelo

Most people accept a vision of themselves that is simply too small by conforming to the small visions of those around them.
Titans live for a vision larger than themselves. Whether it may be religious, civil, political, artistic, entrepreneurial, Titans are those who made great personal sacrifices for what they believed to be a vision larger than themselves: Jesus, Nelson Mandela, Gandhi, Martin Luther King, Mother Theresa, Abraham Lincoln, Picasso, Richard Branson, Steve Jobs, Barack Obama, the list goes on!
Richard Branson said, *"My interest in life comes from setting myself huge, apparently unachievable challenges and trying to rise above them."*
Barack Obama stated, *"It's only when you hitch your wagon to something larger than yourself that you realize your true potential."*
And Patanjali said, *"When you are inspired by some great purpose, some extraordinary project, all your thoughts break their bonds: Your mind transcends limitations, your consciousness expands in every direction, and you find yourself in a new, great and wonderful world. Dormant*

forces, faculties and talents become alive, and you discover yourself to be a greater person by far than you ever dreamed yourself to be."

By having a vision larger than yourself, it will inherently force you to think and act in a larger context, and you will develop new capabilities you didn't know you had.

A Titan Vision Connects You To Your Future.

"If you see more continuity between yourself now and yourself in the future, you probably put more value on delayed rewards and less value on immediate rewards."

– Walter Mischel

Most people can't connect to their future selves because they don't have a Titan Vision of themselves. They see their future selves as complete strangers. They have an 'I'll-deal-with-you-tomorrow' type of mentality. This is why most people don't eat healthy food, don't exercise regularly, and don't save any money.

When connected with your future self in the present, you will be much more likely to stay disciplined and delay gratification in the present, and do the things that will be in your future self's best interest. You will be willing to sacrifice more of your present pleasures for the sake of your future self.

How we think about the future is a key driver of our happiness, health, as well as success in school, work, and life in general. When we have a Titan Vision, our life is good! We feel excited! Our happiness and health increase. We feel like life's worth living! On the other hand, when we're not hopeful of our future, things turn in the opposite direction.

We feel demotivated. We lack energy. And life seems like a drag.

Your ability to connect with *your Titan Vision fires you up in the present!*

Here are some benefits of having a Titan Vision:

- **Acts as your "North Star."** It gives you a mental picture of a brighter future you can't simply let go.
- **You go to bed at night anticipating** the next day and wake up in the morning excited and ready to live out your vision.
- **Brings enthusiasm, optimism and happiness to your life.** As Paulo Coelho said, *"It's the possibility of having a dream come true that makes life interesting."*
- Increases your odds of **becoming successful**.
- Makes life **worth living**.
- **Less willpower and self-discipline** needed.
- Increases your **productivity**.
- Improves your **health and well-being**.
- Helps you **live longer!**

T

TITAN FOCUS

"He that too much embraceth holds little."
– Romanian proverb

Now that you have your life dreams written down on your list, it's important to rediscover *what's truly important to you.* At the end of your life, it won't be the Rolls-Royces and Ferraris that matter the most to you, but the following:

1. Did you have the courage to follow your dreams?

2. Who did you become as a person, father, husband, professional, friend?

3. Did you find joy in life?

4. Did your life bring joy to others?

5. Did you leave this world better than you found it?

Considering that a lifetime is, by definition, limited in time, you must narrow down the dreams you would like to accomplish. Cut your list down to your five most important dreams. These are your Titan 5 for Life. What are the five most important things you must have accomplished at the end of your life for you to say, 'I lived an extraordinary life?'

No worries, my ambitious friend! If you accomplish your Titan 5 for Life way before your deathbed, you might always add other dreams, but it's important that you start with no more than five.

Imagine you have five plants and enough water for those five plants. If you tried to water ten plants with the same amount of water, you would have less water for each plant. Consequently, they would grow much more slowly. Some might even die because of not getting enough water! Well, these plants represent your dreams. The water represents your energy and time. So narrow down your list! As Bill Gates said, *"My success, part of it certainly, is that I have focused in on a few things."*

Build your life around your Titan 5 for Life. Focus on them like a Titan!

Why A Titan Focus?

"The successful warrior is the average man,
with laser-like focus."

– Bruce Lee

Any Titan achievement is not a coincidence. It's always the result of a clearly defined focus, meticulous planning and consistent execution. But it all starts with a Titan Focus.

A Titan Focus gives you clarity. And clarity is the DNA of a Titan Life.

In July 1991, Bill Gates, Sr. invited his son Bill Gates, Jr., the founder of Microsoft, and investor Warren Buffett over for dinner. Bill Gates, Sr. asked his guests: "What factor do you feel has been the most important in getting to where you've gotten in life?" Buffett immediately replied, "Focus." Bill Gates, Jr. agreed.

Focus is more valuable than intelligence. There are so many "brilliant" people who never amount to anything. And there are people with average intelligence who build Titan Lives, thanks entirely to their ability to focus!

Your focus drives your behavior. As the saying goes, *"Where focus goes, energy flows, and results show."* If you focus on getting bigger biceps, you will work on your biceps. The result, you will get bigger biceps!

A focus on your Titan 5 for Life empowers you with wisdom to make those judgments effectively. If your priorities grow out of your Titan 5 for Life, if they are deeply planted in your heart and in your mind, you will spend most of your time working on making your Titan 5 for Life a reality. And you will do so with Titan enthusiasm!

The Age Of Distraction.

"Until a man selects a definite purpose in life, he dissipates his energies and spreads his thoughts over so many subjects and in so many different directions that they lead not to power, but to indecision and weakness."

– Napoleon Hill

We live in the age of distraction. We receive notifications from emails, texts, social media and calls all day long. Only those who can *focus* can have a *Titan Life*.

Forget about all the projects you want to accomplish. Focus only on the one you are developing now!

Steve Jobs said, *"That's been one of my mantras – focus and simplicity. Simple can be harder than complex: You have to work hard to get your thinking clean to make it simple. But it's worth it in the end because once you get there, you can move mountains."*

Alexander Graham Bell stated, *"Concentrate all your thoughts upon the work at hand. The sun's rays do not burn until brought to a focus."*

And Stefan Zweig said, *"Concentration is the eternal secret of every mortal achievement."*

Titans know that it's preferable to be Titan at a few things rather than mediocre at multiple things.

Multitasking is the Enemy.

"You do something all day long, don't you? Everyone does. If you get up at seven o'clock and go to bed at eleven, you have put in sixteen good hours, and it is certain with most men, that they have been doing something all the time. They have been either walking, or reading, or writing, or thinking. The only trouble is that they do it about a great many things and I do it about one. If they took the time in question and applied it in one direction, to one object, they would succeed. Success is sure to follow such application. The trouble lies in the fact that people do not have an object, one thing, to which they stick, letting all else go. Success is the product of the severest kind of mental and physical application."

– Thomas A. Edison

We live in a world that celebrates and almost reveres multitasking.

When you multitask, instead of channeling your complete focus into one task, *you spread it thin.* This prevents you from diving deep into any of your tasks. The result, poorer outcomes, and thus, less gratification.

While most people scatter their focus, Titans *focus on one thing at a time.*

If some of your Titan 5 for Life are "to have my own family," "to become a best-selling author" and "to learn to play the piano," it's important that you don't scatter your focus by multitasking. It's best to focus on one thing at a time, so *you can give your undivided attention to each different thing.*

Titan 5 For Life Vs. "Urgent".

"Most of us spend too much time on what is urgent and not enough time on what is important."

– Stephen Covey

It's easy to get caught in a flood of minutiae. We all have "urgent" matters that require our immediate attention.

The key to a Titan Life *is to stay focused on your Titan 5 for Life rather than what is most "urgent."*

Your Titan 5 for Life are the things you must do to have a Titan Life, but somehow they seldom get done because they are not "urgent": exercising when you are healthy, writing your book when you already have another source of income, reading when there is no one to test your knowledge, nurturing your relationships when you "believe" they will be there tomorrow. Sure, Titans also have crises and emergencies that require their immediate attention, but the number is relatively small.

One strategy to having a Titan Life is *to proactively treat your Titan 5 for Life as "life and death,"* even though they may not seem so in the moment… But they will when you get to your deathbed!

Simplify, Simplify, Simplify…

"Concentrate. Narrow down. Exclude."

– Henry Miller

What's going on in your life that's not part of your Titan 5 for Life? All that stuff is wasting your time, pulling your attention from what's important.

As much as possible, simplify your life by eliminating the stuff that's not on your short list, or minimizing it.

First, see what can be *eliminated*. Next, see what can be *automated*. And last, *delegate* the things that cannot be eliminated or automated.

The key to a Titan Life is *to be productive, not busy*. Do less meaningless work, so you can focus on your Titan goals.

Another thing to ask yourself is, *"Are you inventing things to do to avoid the important?"*

Your Most Valuable Asset.

"A man who dares to waste one hour of time has not discovered the value of life."
— *Charles Darwin*

What is your most valuable asset? Think about it. Is it your health? You can be healthy, then get sick, and then regain your health. Is it your money? You can lose all your money, and then you can make it all back. Is it your spouse? Your spouse might mean everything to you. And yet, 50% of married people get divorced, and then find a new spouse that is suddenly the love of their life. How about your friends? Friends are important, and yet, how many friends have you had through your life you no longer keep in touch with?

Your most valuable asset is *time*. You can never lose time and get it back again. You can't spend time and then go earn more. You can't buy it, rent it, nor borrow it...

Time is the great equalizer. Whether rich or poor, young or old, we all have the same 24 hours in a day. How you spend your time will determine your destiny. Titans respect their time. They leverage it and use it appropriately.

Use your time wisely, and you'll enjoy a Titan Life. Squander your time, and it will be gone forever!

Learn To Say "No."

"People think focus means saying yes to the thing you've got to focus on. But that's not what it means at all. It means saying no to the hundred other good ideas that there are. You have to pick carefully. I'm actually as proud of the things we haven't done as the things I have done."

– Steve Jobs

Do you ever feel like you don't have enough time? *Lack of time is lack of priorities.*

One secret to having a Titan Life is *to focus on your Titan 5 for Life and say "no" to the rest.* Titans say "no" almost to everything.

Most people and companies fail because they focus on too many "opportunities." Ubiquity kills a company and the human spirit. Don't dilute your focus with other opportunities. *Being selective – doing less – is the path of Titans.*

The only way to free up time for your Titan 5 for Life is to have the courage to say "no" to the rest. You don't have to be rude, but you have to be honest, especially with yourself. You either spend your every hour at the whim of other people's expectations or you live your Titan Life. A simple "it's not going to work for me" will do. You'll find this liberating!

Please remember that you're always saying "no" to something anyway. *When you say "yes" to the apparently urgent things in your life, you say "no" to your Titan 5 for Life.*

A Plan B Is The Enemy.

*"Singleness of purpose is one of the chief essentials for success
in life, no matter what may be one's aim."*
– *John D. Rockefeller*

Most parents tell their children that "having a plan B is necessary in case their plan A fails." While this may seem like the reasonable thing to do, Titans have no plan B! They know that having a Plan B will only sabotage your plan A.

Failing is part of the process of a Titan. For Titans, while experimenting temporary defeat is part of the journey, but *permanent failure is not an option!* They focus on one thing until successful or until *they decide* they are through or no longer interested.

So, what do Titans do when they decide that they are through or no longer interested? *They look for the next plan A!* But they never start a plan A with a plan B in mind!

When in 1519, the explorer Hernán Cortés landed in Mexico to begin his great conquest, he gave the order to his men to burn the ships. Why? Because he knew that *retreat is easy when you have a plan B!*

Will you have a plan-B spouse in case your marriage with your current spouse does not go as expected?

If you have a plan B, it will eventually become your plan A!

Concentrate.

*"Concentrate every minute like a Roman – like a man – on
doing what's in front of you with precise and genuine
seriousness, tenderly, willingly, with justice. And on freeing
yourself from all other distractions. Yes, you can – if you do
everything as if it were the last thing you were doing in your
life, and stop being aimless, stop letting your emotions override
what your mind tells you, stop being hypocritical, self-centered,
irritable. You see how few things you have to do to live a*

satisfying and reverent life? If you can manage this, that's all even the gods can ask of you."

– Marcus Aurelius

Only those who can *concentrate* on a single task at a time can have a Titan Life.

Most people feel scattered and distracted and assume they should be able to concentrate easily. And if not, there must be something wrong with them, and, therefore, they should be medicated. But this would be the same as assuming that you can be an Olympic weightlifter from the get-go! Like with anything else, *concentration takes practice.*

As weightlifting doesn't just make you strong for lifting weights, but it also makes your body strong for everything you do the rest of the day, *concentration practice* strengthens your ability to focus for everything you do in your life.

To practice concentration, simply bring your focus onto a single task. If anything pulls your attention away – which will happen, especially initially – you calmly and gently guide it back to the focus point.

Think of it as doing repetitions with weights. To build strong muscles, you lift the weights up and down repeatedly. Each time you do it, you get a tiny bit stronger, and over a long period you get a lot stronger. *It's the repetition that is key.* Eventually, you can lift a very large weight.

The same thing goes for concentration. Your mind wanders, you bring it back to the object of focus. Each time you bring your mind back to the object of focus, your concentration gets a tiny bit stronger, and over a long period it gets a lot stronger. It's the *repetition* that eventually brings a Titan Focus.

By daily practice of concentration, your focus, too, can develop to Titan proportions, and without the help of any medication!

T

TITAN PLAN

"A goal without a plan is just a wish."
— Antoine de Saint-Exupéry

Now that you have your Titan 5 for Life clearly defined and written down, it's important that you make specific plans for each one of them. Otherwise, they will just remain "dreams."

Titans throughout history have used planning to prepare for the future.

Benjamin Franklin said, *"By failing to prepare, you are preparing to fail."*

Alan Lakein wrote, *"Planning is bringing the future into the present so that you can do something about it now."*

And Eleanor Roosevelt stated, *"It takes as much energy to wish as it does to plan."*

A Titan Life does not respond to wishes or dreams, but to Titan plans, backed by a Titan Focus through consistent Titan Action.

The Unplanned Life...

"The typical human life seems to be quite unplanned, undirected, unlived, and unsavored. Only those who consciously think about the adventure of living as a matter of making choices among options, which they have found for themselves, ever establish real self-control and live their lives fully."
— Karl Albrecht

Even if you know exactly what your Titan 5 for Life are, you will never achieve them unless you have a Titan Plan by which to attain said goals. A lack of planning, regardless of the endeavor, inevitably leads to a failure.

It's interesting to me that most people spend more time planning their vacations than their lives. No wonder there are so many people wandering aimlessly through life.

As Jim Rohn said, *"If you don't design your own life plan, chances are you'll fall into someone else's plan. And guess what they have planned for you? Not much."*

Your Plan Is Your Servant, Not Your Master.

"In preparing for battle I have always found that plans are useless, but planning is indispensable."
– Dwight D. Eisenhower

A Titan Plan is not an exact road map, but a compass. It gives you *a sense of direction.*

Life does not always move in straight lines. It moves more like a winding river. You can only see to the next bend, and only when you reach that next turn can you see more. But it's important we have a sense of where the river is going!

A Titan Plan is about *constant redesigning and tweaking.* What worked yesterday might not necessarily work today.

Another thing to consider is you must make sure that your Titan Plan works for *you.* It should be tailored to your style, your needs, your particular ways. If the plan is not working for you, go back to the drawing board!

Assign Imminent Deadlines.

"A goal is a dream with a deadline."
– Napoleon Hill

Parkinson's Law states that *work expands in perceived importance and complexity in relation to the time allotted for its completion.*

This means that if you give yourself a week to complete a two-hour task, then – psychologically speaking – the task will increase in complexity and become more daunting to fill that week. It may not even fill the extra time with more work, but just stress and tension about having to get it done.

Use Parkinson's Law to accomplish more in less time. *Shrink your mental deadlines.* If you believe that something will take you an hour to do, give yourself 45 minutes instead.

By assigning an imminent deadline, *you will be forced to work faster and focus more.* The task will psychologically reduce in complexity. This is the magic of the imminent deadline!

Backward Planning.

*"For tomorrow belongs to the people
who prepare for it today."*
– *African proverb*

Backward planning is one of the best productivity tools you can use to make your Titan 5 for Life a reality.

The idea is to start with your ultimate objective – your Titan 5 for Life – and then work backward from there to develop your plan.

Backward planning differs from traditional planning. You must force yourself to think from a completely new perspective, to help you see things you might miss if you use traditional planning.

By starting at the end and looking back, you can prepare yourself for success, map out the milestones you need to reach, and realize where in your plan you have to be particularly gritty or creative to achieve the desired outcome.

Break Down your Goals.

"The secret of getting ahead is getting started. The secret of getting started is breaking your complex overwhelming tasks into small manageable tasks, and starting on the first one."
— *Mark Twain*

A Titan Plan breakdowns your Titan 5 for Life into smaller, actionable goals.

Let's say you want to write a book. Writing a book may seem like a daunting task, especially for someone who has never written a book. So how do you actually write a book? One chapter at a time. How do you write a chapter? One paragraph at a time. How do you write a paragraph? One word at a time!

Unless you breakdown your Titan 5 for Life into smaller, actionable goals, you will never get there because your Titan 5 for Life may look so unsurmountable that it becomes discouraging to even start!

By breaking down your goals, not only will you be working on actionable goals, but you will also build *momentum* with each small victory you will achieve.

Since you already have your Titan 5 for Life, ask yourself:
- What are my Titan 5 for the Next 10 Years?
- What are my Titan 5 for the Next 3 Years?
- What are my Titan 5 for the Year?
- What are my Titan 5 for the Quarter?
- What are my Titan 5 for the Month?
- What are my Titan 5 for the Week?
- What are my Titan 5 for Today?

As Jay-Z said, *"We made short and long-term projections, we kept it realistic, but the key thing is that we wrote it down, which is as important as visualization in realizing success."*

Plan Your Week.

"The week gives you the most manageable perspective."
— Stephen Covey

Planning your week is the blueprint for a Titan week! It gives you a sense of direction and purpose to the way you spend each day.

Your mind needs a trusting system to focus your actions; otherwise, it gets distracted with other issues.

The week has 168 hours! It has work days, evenings, the weekend. It's close enough to be relevant, but distant enough to provide perspective.

Planning your week, once a week, before the week begins, is one of the most powerful strategies to help you find harmony and increase your productivity. In addition, it will put you in touch with your Titan 5 for Life by setting daily goals and scheduling activities for each one of your Titan 5 for Life.

Yes, you can still adapt and prioritize daily as needed. But it will be easier to get back on track since you already know where your week is heading!

The best time to plan your week is Sunday morning.

How to Plan Your Week.

"It's not the will to win that matters. Everyone has it.
It's the will to prepare to win that matters."
— Coach Bear Bryant.

On Sunday morning, while the rest of the house sleeps, take one or two hours of solitude. (Please, turn off your devices!) This is the time to craft your Titan Week! Here are the Titan steps:

1. **Review** your Titan 5 for Life, Titan 5 for the Next 10 Years, Titan 5 for the Next 3 Years, Titan 5 for the Year, Titan 5 for the Quarter and Titan 5 for the Month.

2. **Review your past week.** Journal about it. Write a paragraph for each individual day. This way, you will start noticing patterns. Did you achieve your Titan 5 from the past week? Check off the items you achieved. Ideally, you have achieved all your Titan 5 for the Week. If not, learn why you didn't achieve them, and make sure you achieve them in the upcoming week.

3. Write three **Titan Victories** from the past week. Write three **Titan Lessons** from the past week. Ask yourself, *'What do I need to improve in the upcoming week?'*

4. **Plan the week ahead.** Remember to include not only your business meetings, but also your family time, workouts, reading, hobbies, wake-up time, meals, supplements, naps, bedtime, even your free time. What gets scheduled gets done! You might say that your family is important to you, but why aren't they on your schedule? Or, you might say that your health is important, but your schedule says otherwise. As Stephen Covey said, *"The key is not to prioritize what's on your schedule, but to schedule your priorities."*

Harmony in life comes down to weekly planning.

Daily Planning.

"Never begin the day until it is finished on paper."
– Jim Rohn

It's important to reflect on what we want to achieve *before we start our day.*

In the same way that making a grocery list will make you enjoy your shopping because you won't have to remember what you had to buy, planning your day will make you focus on the really important things, so you can enjoy the process.

By simply taking 5-10 minutes each morning to strategically plan out your day, you'll be able to get significantly more out of your day.

Titans are highly organized. They know that if they don't schedule their days, other people's priorities will infuse their days.

If you look at Bill Gates or Elon Musk, they plan their days in 5-minute intervals. Other Titans plan their days in 15-minute chunks. I recommend you start with planning your days in *30-minute intervals.*

So plan your day, and don't forget to sprinkle simple pleasures throughout your day!

Titan 5 for Today Vs. Tasks & Errands.

"The secret of all victory lies in the organization of the non obvious."
– Marcus Aurelius

Your Titan 5 for Today are not to be confused with your Tasks & Errands.

Your Titan 5 for Today contribute to taking you closer to your Titan 5 for the Week, which take you closer to your Titan 5 for the Month, which take you closer to your Titan 5 for the Quarter, which take you closer to your Titan 5 for the Year, which take you closer to your Titan 5 for the Next 3 Years, which take you closer to your Titan 5 for the Next 10 Years, which take you closer to your Titan 5 for Life!

Your Tasks & Errands are not necessarily related to your Titan 5 for Life, but are things we all have to do: buying groceries, picking up your shirt from the dry-cleaners, you get the idea.

The problem is when you give priority to your Tasks & Errands, instead of your Titan 5 for Today.

Divide your day in Titan 5 for Today and Tasks & Errands, and tackle your Titan 5 for Today first. Next, tackle your Tasks & Errands, for example, after 4:00 PM or 5:00 PM, when your energy levels are low.

In addition, try batching your Tasks & Errands. For example: check your emails and reply to them once or twice a day all together, set a time to return all your calls, set a day to check your mail once a week. This way, you'll be more efficient as you will minimize the mental burden of task switching.

Always ask yourself, *"Will this further my Titan 5 for Life?"* If not, it's a task or errand!

Other Titan Tips For Planning.

- **Get a planner.** Have it in front of you at all times. Freedom comes from a stable life.

- **Schedule your family trips** in January for the entire year and arrange your life around those family vacations.

- **Schedule time with the people you love.** Have a family day, at least once a week.

- **Plan your weekly date** with your spouse or partner.
- **Schedule alone time**.
- **Plan breaks through the day:** meditation, naps, breathing, snacks, meals, free time.
- **Set up a start time and a finish time**, with constant breaks. You will become more productive!
- **Commune with nature**, at least once a week.
- **Plan your weekly meals**. If you're "too busy to cook," cook all your weekly meals on Sunday, so you just have to heat them up during the week. Your health and finances will thank you!
- **Plan your grocery shopping day.** Go grocery shopping at unusual times. You will go in and come out more quickly. Besides, you will enjoy the shopping experience more!
- **Leave space around things in your day.** Don't stack appointments or tasks back to back.
- **Plan your weekly cleaning day.** Use Parkinson's Law to do everything as quickly as possible!
- **Don't forget to schedule times for fun** as well!
- **Take a few minutes in the morning** to review your daily schedule and plan for a Titan day!

T

TITAN HABITS

"Successful people are simply those with successful habits."
— Brian Tracy

Success comes from what we do daily, not from occasional home runs.

For thousands of years, success in human life has been studied by great thinkers and philosophers. They all seem to agree that the secret to becoming a Titan is not talent or willpower, but Titan Habits.

Your outcomes in life result from your habits. Who you are today results directly from the habits you have formed in the past. So *to have a better you in the future, you must form new, better habits in the present.*

By forming Titan Habits, you, too, can become successful and live a Titan Life.

Consistency of Purpose.

"Long term consistency will always
trump short term intensity."

— Bruce Lee

The key to a Titan Life is *consistency*. A Titan Life does not come about from what you do sometimes. It results from consistent effort toward your goals.

Consistency of purpose is the mother of mastery. You may be very talented, but unless you pay the price day in and day out, you will never achieve a Titan Life.

Be constantly taking action! Cement a little each day! It's about what you do *most of the time.* Let me give you an example:

Let's say you and your significant other brush your teeth every evening before going to bed. One day, you are both lying in bed, enjoying a great conversation. A couple of hours go by and you both now feel sleepy. You kiss each other good night and forget – or decide not – to brush your teeth that night. What do you think will happen to your oral hygiene? Nothing major! Because what matters is *what you do most of the time.* And most of the time – most evenings – you do brush your teeth!

The same can be said about your Titan Goals. When you take action daily, even if you slack or decide to take a break on a particular day to play with your son, you will still be well on your way to achieving your Titan Goals because what matters is what you do *most of the time.* And most of the time, you take action toward your goals!

However, make it a rule *never to skip two days in a row,* unless it's part of your Titan Recovery period (more on this in a later chapter!).

Start Small.

"Be faithful in small things because it is in them that your strength lies."

– Mother Teresa

Most people fail at installing new habits because they set these huge goals that are neither actionable nor sustainable, at least initially. These are the people who are trying to achieve "overnight success." And a Titan Life is never an overnight success!

Every new Titan Habit you want to install must start off small. For instance, if you do not have the habit of going to the gym daily, don't set your goal to go to the gym five days a week for an hour each time! Instead, plan to go to the gym three times a week, for fifteen minutes each time. Or if you do not have the habit of reading daily, don't set your goal to read a book a week! Instead, plan to read two pages three nights a week.

What matters is that you *get in the habit* of going to the gym or reading. Quickly, you'll be wanting to go to the gym and read for either longer sessions or more frequently!

Small, consistent action, over time, form Titan habits.

Habits Work Like Compound Interest.

"Understanding both the power of compound interest and the difficulty of getting it is the heart and soul of understanding a lot of things."
– Charlie Munger

Habits, like compound interest, only accumulate over time. That's when you will see the results!

Titan results do not come overnight! You must be patient and confident that your Titan habits, when done consistently, will lead you to Titan results in the future, even when you do not see any apparent results in the present!

And that's the thing about Titan Habits. You have to *trust* that, if you plant seeds day in and day out, the results will "suddenly" come. Because they will come!

Let's say Mary and Christine are best friends. After going to the beach with their friend Victoria and seeing, firsthand, how amazing she looks, they – Mary and Christine – decide to go to a gym together. They pay the most expensive gym membership they can afford, consciously or subconsciously, thinking that the more expensive the gym membership is, the better the equipment will be and, therefore, the faster the results will come! They buy new workout clothes and gear and go to the gym five days a week! Three weeks later, Christine, upon not seeing any *visible* results, quits. So long to the new workout clothes and gear! Mary, who has also been reading about the importance of consistency, keeps coming to the gym five days a week. Christine gets transferred to another city for work. A year later, Christine is back home for Christmas, and she meets Mary for coffee. To Christine's astonishment, Mary looks amazing! Christine, being a good friend, tells Mary so. Mary, surprised, says: "Thank you!" To Christine's eyes, Mary has become an "overnight success"! Christine now inquires about the type of diet she is following, whether she eats carbs or not, her supplements, her "secrets." Mary, flattered, does not know what to say. What Christine fails to realize is that Mary kept "compounding interest" by going to the gym day after day. At the same time, Mary is surprised because she sees little change in herself. She kind of notices that her waist is slimmer – this is why she now uses a smaller pants size, but that's about it.

Like your savings account, your growth can be quite remarkable when you look back at what or where you used to be. Even though your savings account is constantly growing, you do not notice its growth from day to day. Even when making progress, you may not notice your own improvement. How fast or how slow should not be your concern; what matters is that you're moving forward! Your savings account grows faster or slower, depending on the economic cycle. You also have "cycles" where growth accelerates, but it's slower at other times. Yet, *as long as you take consistent action, you will always be growing!*

Do not be discouraged by what you perceive as your lack of growth. If you have not given up, then you are growing. You just may not see it until much later!

Installing A New Habit.

*"We are what we repeatedly do. Excellence,
then, is not an act, but a habit."*
– Aristotle

Installing a Titan Habit is harder than installing a bad habit. The reason is simple. While the reward of a bad habit is immediate (eating a doughnut, smoking a cigarette), the reward of a Titan Habit is delayed (eating healthy, working out, writing a book).

From an evolutionary perspective, *we humans are wired to want immediate payoffs.* We want things now rather than later! In prehistoric times the availability of food was uncertain. This is why our instinct, like other animals, is to seize the reward at hand (food, water, sex) to survive. And resisting this instinct is hard! Our tendency is to grab the smaller, immediate reward and skip the larger but delayed reward.

Installing a Titan Habit is always hard initially. It's hard because it is a disruption of your neurobiology. You must recode your brain. *You must break the patterns of your natural instincts or the ones you have acquired, sometimes, for years!* The old part of you must die and the new part of you must be born. And like with any birth, it hurts! Ask any mother.

According to University College London, *it takes an average of 66 days of daily action to install a new habit.* After 66 days, according to the research, it becomes automatic and easier to do the new habit than not to do it. You don't have think about it. It becomes second nature.

Installing a new habit may be compared to the launching of a space shuttle. In the initial stage, the space shuttle uses the greatest amount of fuel because it needs to conquer the forces of gravity. In the second stage, the space shuttle has already conquered the initial forces of gravity, but interestingly enough, this is when most space shuttle accidents happen. In the third and final stage, momentum kicks in, and the space shuttle glides easily, without using much fuel.

Similarly, in the initial stage is when we need to use more willpower (fuel) to conquer our already ingrained habits (forces of gravity). In the second stage, this is when we "think" that we don't have to use that much willpower, but upon seeing no apparent results, you start questioning yourself. *'What's the point of doing this? 'This isn't working.' 'Why bother?'* This is the stage where you're most likely to "fall" (when most accidents happen). But if you press through like a Titan, you will build momentum, and you get to the third and final stage where all the hard work, sacrifice and suffering pay off as the new habit that you've been working on integrates at a spiritual, mental, physical and emotional level. It becomes part of who you are (without using much fuel!). You come out more skilled and in better touch with your Titan self.

Don't give up! What's hard today will become easier tomorrow with practice!

Build Your Titan System.

"When I'm in writing mode for a novel, I get up at 4:00 am and work for five to six hours. In the afternoon, I run for 10km or swim for 1500m (or do both), then I read a bit and listen to some music. I go to bed at 9:00 pm. I keep to this routine every day without variation. The repetition itself becomes the important thing; it's a form of mesmerism. I mesmerize myself to reach a deeper state of mind. But to hold to such repetition for so long — six months to a year — requires a good amount of mental and physical strength. In that sense, writing a long novel is like survival training. Physical strength is as necessary as artistic sensitivity."

– Haruki Murakami

Everyone has dreams. Titans build systems to achieve them.

Most people focus on the goal. Titans focus on the process, the systems! They only check on the goal occasionally – once a week – to make sure they are on the right track, but they focus on the processes, the systems that help them achieve their Titan results.

If you look at the most successful people, companies, and sport clubs around the world, they all have built, whether consciously or unconsciously, regular and reliable routines that cause their Titan results. Here are a few examples:

Barcelona FC's Youth Academy	Serena Williams	Oprah Winfrey
6:45 AM – Wake up & Breakfast.	7:00 AM – Breakfast.	7:10 AM – Wake up.
7:30 AM – Off to school.	8:00 AM – Tennis Practice.	8:00 AM – Take the dogs out. Make
8:00 AM – School.	12:00 PM – Lunch	coffee. Read five
2:00 PM – Lunch.	Break.	quotes.
3:00 PM – Soccer-related conference.	2:00 PM – Strength Training.	8:30 AM – Spiritual exercises. Sufi
3:30 PM – English lesson.	4:00 PM – Dance Class.	reading. Meditation. 9:00 AM –
4:00 PM – Baccalaureate lesson.	5:00 PM – Rehab.	Workout. 10:30 AM –
5:00 PM – Training starts.	6:00 PM – Dinner with Family.	Business Meetings (or gardening if it's
8:00 PM – Free time.	8:00 PM – Social Media and	Thursday!)
9:00 PM – Dinner.	Promotional	12:30 PM – Lunch.
9:30 PM – Free Time.	Work.	1:30 PM – Business
10:30 PM – Bedtime.	12:00 AM – Sleep.	meetings.
		3:30 PM – Some form of exercise.
		4:30 PM – Tea and reading.
		6:00 PM – Dinner & take the dogs out.
		7:00 PM – Spend time with loved ones.
		9:30 PM – Bath, gratitude & bedtime.

As you can see, Titans have systems, so if on a particular day, they don't feel "inspired" or "motivated," they still do it because *they follow the system.*

If you want to be a Titan soccer player, do what Titan soccer players do. If you want to become a Titan tennis player, do what Titan tennis players do. And if you want to be a Titan media mogul, learn about the routines of Titan media moguls!

Developing Titan systems is how to build your Titan Life. So when you get out of bed, you already know what to expect. Develop a system for all aspects of your life: spirit, mind, body, heart, skill, environment, finances, and in everything you do, don't forget about your legacy!

I heard Sylvester Stallone once say at a writer's seminar in Los Angeles he writes every day. He wakes up at 4:30 a.m. and writes for three straight hours, every single day. Even if he has nothing to write, he still sits there for the full amount of time.

A Titan system matters! Most people put much effort into getting their goals, but *unless you build a Titan System that will allow you to be consistent*, you will never get there! The system works because you work the system. So don't forget to take action!

Wake Up Early!

"It is well to be up before daybreak, for such habits contribute to health, wealth, and wisdom."
– Aristotle

Titans wake up early.

Thomas Jefferson said, *"The sun has not caught me in bed in fifty years."*

Jonathan Swift said, *"I never knew a man come to greatness or eminence who lay abed late in the morning."*

And Benjamin Franklin said, *"The early morning has gold in its mouth."*

The only way to accomplish Titan things in life and be in charge of your destiny is if you wake up early. While the rest of the world is asleep, *you have an average of an hour or 90 minutes of advantage above the rest.*

When you wake up early, you put "mind over mattress." And this gives you the first victory of the day! *It sets you up for discipline and success.* This discipline will give you the same courage to go to the gym, talk to customers, make difficult phone calls, read, and eat healthy food.

The Power of Morning & Evening Rituals.

"Think in the morning, act in the noon,
read in the evening, and sleep at night."
– William Blake

There are two parts of your day you can always control: your morning and your evening. All hell can break loose throughout your day, but you can always control how you *start* your day and how you *finish* it.

The purpose of your *morning ritual* is to prime you for Titan Action, while the purpose of your *evening ritual* is to prime you for Titan Recovery.

Your Titan Morning Ritual.

"How you start your day is how you live your day.
How you live your day is how you live your life."
– Louise Hay

Your Titan Morning Ritual is sacred to your self-mastery, wellbeing and happiness. This is the daily time for you to take your life to the next level in all aspects of life. This is the time for you to work on developing *you.* Each day is a new day and a new opportunity to build a Titan Life. Your Titan Morning Ritual sets the tone for a Titan day.

While most people start their days in a reactive mode (watching the news, checking their cell phones, emails, social media), Titans start their day in a proactive mode, meaning, they're *in charge* of their mornings.

The morning is when you are most impressionable, so you must make sure that you "impress" your brain with the right stuff! Your willpower is highest in the morning, so why start your day with other people's priorities?

Get up at least an hour earlier. This does not mean you will sleep an hour less each night. Quite the opposite! It means you will have to discipline yourself to go to sleep an hour earlier each evening. Here are some Titan strategies:

- **Drink a glass of lukewarm water** with freshly squeezed lemon. (Add a bit of ulmo honey if you can!) Before you do this, brush your teeth and tongue. Otherwise, you will swallow the bacteria you accumulated in your mouth during the night.
- Watch the **sun rise.**
- **Reflect** on your life.
- **Be grateful** for your blessings.
- **Visualize & do affirmations (or pray.)**
- **Read** something inspirational.
- **Plan,** or review, your day.
- **Exercise.**
- **Take a shower.** Alternate hot and cold water.
- **Have a Titan breakfast**.
- **Connect** with your loved ones.

While there's probably not an ideal morning ritual that fits everyone, see what works for you! What matters is that you find *your own Titan Morning Ritual.* While the rest of the world is asleep, give yourself 60-90 minutes for your Titan Morning Ritual. The world needs you to play at your best!

Your Titan Project.

"To change your life, you need to change your priorities."
— Mark Twain

After you do your Titan Morning Ritual, the next thing Titans do is they spend thirty to sixty minutes working on their Titan Project.

Your Titan Project is the one project that will change the game for you – and your family – and that *will not only make a name for you but also generate long-term income and will give you lasting satisfaction and happiness.*

Before working on your Titan Project, make up your mind, concentrate like a professional athlete before a big competition, and ask God, the Universe or your Higher Self for guidance and help. Then, do the work!

Your Titan Evening Ritual.

"End your day with a smile, a happy thought, and a grateful heart."
— Clint Walker

Titans don't wait until the morning to prepare for a Titan day. They start the night before!

The close of each day is just as important as the start. By implementing an evening ritual, you will prepare yourself for the next morning, recharge with a restful night and minimize the resistance you encounter in getting things done.

Around an hour and a half before going to bed, start your Titan Evening Ritual. Here are some Titan strategies:

- **Take a walk after dinner**, ideally through a park or in nature.

- **Turn off your electronic devices** at least ninety minutes before your bedtime.
- **Review your past day.** Anything that you could not achieve today? No worries! Life is not always perfect! Make sure you do it tomorrow!
- **Journal.** Debrief about your day.
- **Celebrate three small victories you achieved.**
- **Plan your next day.** Design the blueprint for a Titan day tomorrow.
- **Take a hot shower or bath** with Epsom salts.
- **Meditate.**
- **Read.**
- **Connect** with your loved ones.
- **Go to bed early.**

Again, while there's probably not an ideal evening ritual that fits everyone, see what works for you! What matters is that you find *your own Titan Evening Ritual.*

T

TITAN ACTION

"Plans are only good intentions unless they immediately degenerate into hard work."

– *Peter Drucker*

A Titan Life is achieved by those who take Titan action.

The bridge between where you are now and where you want to be in the future is built through action.

While most people procrastinate and wait for the "ideal circumstances," Titans take action now. While most people think or talk about acting, Titans act. While most people are busy being busy, Titans are busy working on their Titan 5 for Life. While most people take forever to get educated because they believe they must know every single detail in advance, Titans do "ready, fire, arm!," and then, correct along the way. While most people lack consistency and work when they feel "inspired" or "motivated," Titans show up all the time, whether they feel inspired and motivated or not. As Picasso said, *"Inspiration exists, but it must find you working."*

Titans work very, very hard. They get more done in a day than most people get done in a month. If you work as much as everyone around is working, you are being like most people. And *if you do what most people do, you will get the results that most people get.* So to get the results that only Titans get, you have to work harder than anyone else and "stretch your muscles" so Titan level of work becomes normal.

The path to a Titan Life is a very lonely road. Yes, you will need a Titan Team to get to the top (more on this in a later chapter!), but you must realize that Titans must work even when their team is not around and no one is watching them.

Start Now!

"A journey of a thousand miles must begin with a single step."
– Lao Tzu

Now is the time to start working on your Titan Life because you are younger now than you ever will be again!

Most people take forever to get educated before taking any action. They use their learning and reading as an excuse to prevent them from doing the work. *Titans prepare and research in as short a time as possible, then take action, and then correct along the way.*

If you think about it, what is the point of constantly reading inspiring articles, reading books, and watching motivational videos if you don't use that knowledge? *Knowledge is power, but power is the ability to act on that knowledge.*

Stop waiting for the "perfect circumstances" because they will never come. To accomplish Titan things in life, you must start where you are today, with whatever tools you may have. As you move forward, better tools will appear on your way. As Maya Angelou said, *"Do the best you can until you know better. Then when you know better, do better."*

Get in the game with whatever you've got from wherever you are. Put out your product, write your book, start your foundation, ASAP, and then, tweak as you go.

Don't sit around another year, watching other people live their Titan Lives! Nothing will work until you make it work.

Act With A Sense Of Urgency.

"The trouble is you think you have time."

– Buddha

One of the keys to having a Titan Life is to *act with a sense of urgency.*

Most people have no urgency to create the life of their dreams, no urgency to attain financial freedom, and no urgency to improve their life.

The main problem is that most people are struggling in life, but not enough! They have just enough money to get by, live an average life, and since everyone around them is doing the same, they subconsciously say to themselves, *'why change?'* I call this the *middle-class syndrome*: you're not wealthy enough to have the life of your dreams, but not poor enough to be hungry for more!

To build a Titan Life, *you must develop a sense of urgency.* You must treat your Titan 5 for Life as if they were life and death! They may not seem like "life and death" in the moment, but they will when you get to your deathbed and realize that regrets replaced dreams…

To create a sense of urgency in the present, *you must cultivate an inner drive and desire to get on with the job quickly and do it fast!*

A sense of urgency feels very much like racing against yourself. And once this sense of urgency is ingrained in you, you develop *a bias for action.*

Pablo Picasso had an artistic career of approximately 70 years. His body of work is estimated at about 50,000 works of art in all media. If you do the math, this is about 2 pieces a day, including weekends. However, for paintings specifically, almost all of his works were very fast, and generally, he averaged three per day when he was in painting mode.

Here are some quotes on acting with a sense of urgency you might enjoy:

Leonardo da Vinci said, *"I have been impressed with the urgency of doing. Knowing is not enough; we must apply. Being willing is not enough; we must do."*

Isabel Allende stated, *"From journalism I learned to write under pressure, to work with deadlines, to have limited space and time, to conduct an interview, to find information, to research, and above all, to use language as efficiently as possible and to remember always that there is a reader out there."*

And Malcolm Gladwell said, *"The most successful entrepreneurs not only have courage and imagination, they also have a sense of urgency. They're not willing to wait. They have a burning desire to get something done."*

Be Patient About Seeing the Results.

"It took me 17 years and 114 days to become an overnight success."

– *Leo Messi*

Patience is a Titan quality. James Cameron took 10 years to create Avatar, from idea to final product. Stephen King's novella Carrie was rejected by 30 publishers. And Nelson Mandela served 27 years in prison before he became the president of South Africa.

Most people start a new project or a new year's resolution, and a couple of weeks into it, they quit. Why? Because they don't see any results soon enough! They have been planting seeds, but after seeing that "none of them grew," they pack up and leave! This is why most people flit from interest to interest, never really accomplishing anything.

To live a Titan Life, realize that the last thing to grow on a fruit tree is the *fruit*. Don't judge each day by the harvest you reap, but by the seeds you plant. And, if you continue planting seeds, day in and day out, one day, the sun and the rain will come out, and your plant will grow! As Epictetus said, *"No great thing is created suddenly."*

Be patient, and trust that the results will come... if you put in the work!

Be Patiently Impatient About Building Your Titan Life.

"Be urgent about making the effort, and patient about seeing the results."

– Ralph Marston

You're probably thinking, *'Ok, so I need to act with a sense of urgency, but I also need to be patient?* That's right!

If you are not patient, you'll quit when the results don't come soon. At the same time, if you don't act with a sense of urgency, not worrying about deadlines and constantly reminding yourself that "good things take time," a year will go by and you'll have almost nothing to show for it. The result in both scenarios? You will fail in achieving your Titan 5 for Life.

Here's one of the keys to building a Titan Life: *You must have a sense of urgency about taking action and be patient about seeing the results.*

Plant seeds with a sense of urgency, day in and day out, and wait patiently for the sun and rain to come out. Building a Titan Life is a marathon, but your daily practice is a sprint.

Finish What You Start.

"Resolve to perform what you ought;
perform without fail what you resolve."
— Benjamin Franklin

Finishing is hard for most people, particularly if there are no external penalties. But this is one of the things that separates Titans from most people. While most people dabble with different projects and then drop them when it gets difficult or boring, Titans always finish what they start.

Forget all the projects you want to do. Have the discipline, focus and resolve to complete the one in hand.

There's no easier way to feel fulfilled, confident and worthy than to finish what you started. Your family will be proud, and, most importantly, you will be proud! As Thomas Carlyle said, *"Nothing builds self-esteem and self-confidence like accomplishment."*

When you push through a difficult project, you don't get to the other side; you reach to *the Next Level.* Thus, taking Titan Action is a great practice for character-building.

Practice "Kaizen".

"Continuous improvement is better than delayed perfection."
– Mark Twain

Kaizen is a Japanese word that could be translated as "constant improvement."

More than anything, *kaizen* is an attitude, a commitment to constantly improving all areas of your life (spirit, mind, body, heart, skill, team, environment, finances, legacy). Because small daily improvements, over time, lead to Titan results.

And this is exactly what happened when Dave Brailsford was hired as the new performance director of the British cycling team in 2003.

Since 1908, British cyclists had won just a single gold medal at the Olympic Games and had never won the *Tour de France*. The performance of British cyclists had been so poor that one of the top bike manufacturers in Europe refused to sell bikes to the team because they were afraid that it would hurt sales if other professionals saw the British cyclists using their gear. What made Dave different from previous coaches was his relentless commitment to *kaizen*.

Dave and his coaches redesigned the bike seats to make them more comfortable. They rubbed alcohol on the tires for a better grip. They tested various fabrics in a wind tunnel to see which one was more aerodynamic. They tested different types of massage oil to see which one led to the fastest muscle recovery. They hired a sleep coach to determine the pillows and mattresses that led to the best night's sleep for each cyclist. They hired a doctor to teach each cyclist the best way to wash their hands to reduce the chances of catching a cold.

These and other small improvements accumulated and
to Titan results faster than anyone could have imagined! Ju.
five years after Dave took over, the British cycling team won
an astounding 60 percent of the gold medals available at the
2008 Olympic Games in Beijing. Four years later, at the
Olympic Games in London, the British cyclists set nine
Olympic records and seven world records. That same year,
Bradley Wiggins became the first British cyclist to win the
Tour de France. The next year, his teammate Chris Froome
won the race, and he would win again in 2015, 2016 and
2017. And, the next year, Geraint Thomas, another
teammate, also won the race, giving the British team six
Tour de France victories in seven years!

Make today better than yesterday! *Commit to improve all
aspects of your life 1 percent at a time.* These will
accumulate and lead you to Titan results!

Focus On The Process.

"When walking, walk. When eating, eat."
– Zen proverb

Most people think they will be happy when they have
achieved this or that. But that is not the case!

Research on *hedonic adaptation* shows we adapt quickly
after reaching our goals. We may be happy for a few days,
but after that, we will be about as happy (or unhappy!) as
before reaching the goal. That's why *we must not tie our
happiness to the outcome, but to the process.* Otherwise, you
will give up before you attain the desired outcome.

Titans are not those who constantly sacrifice pleasure by
imagining the day they will finally get to become a Titan.
Titans are those who focus on the satisfaction they feel every

step forward or accumulate a new piece of

y engaged in hard work when we feel like
gress. *By setting and achieving small*
...uity, we tap into a constant flow of immediate
gratification which keeps us motivated in pursuit of our
long-term goal.

One of the secrets to a Titan Life is not about delaying gratification, but about *discovering gratification along the way.* Therefore, focus on the process, not the final result!

Keep a Victory Logbook.

"Remember to celebrate milestones
as you prepare for the road ahead."

– Nelson Mandela

Success is a series of small victories. Celebrating your small victories is one of the best things you can do to live a Titan Life!

When you experience even small amounts of success, your brain releases dopamine, which is connected to feelings of pleasure, learning and motivation. When you feel the effects of dopamine, you are eager to repeat the actions that resulted in success in the first place. This is why achieving small goals – and celebrating them! - is such an effective way to build *momentum* to stay on track with your long-term goals.

If you are constantly looking ahead and never taking the time to celebrate your accomplishments, you will most likely get burned out. And when you get burned out, you will lose the motivation to stay focused on your long-term goals.

By celebrating and keeping a logbook of your victories, no matter how small, you get to savor your accomplishments and keep track of your progress. And the more you savor your victories and keep track of your progress, the less you will need the applause of other people – because you get to applaud yourself for your own accomplishments –, and the more fuel you will get to build *momentum* and achieve your long-term goals.

Sam Walton said, *"Celebrate your successes. Find some humor in your failures."*

Richard Branson stated, *"If you set daily goals and work through your list every day, you can mark off every completed task with a satisfying tick. This helps keep you motivated to aim for the big targets."*

And Oprah Winfrey said, *"The more you celebrate your life, the more there is in life to celebrate."*

A Victory Logbook should be separate from your journal. This is the place where you will "only" write about your victories, whether big or small. Write about how wonderful it felt to achieve X milestone. In the end, no one else understands what it took to accomplish it!

When you have a record of the progress you have made in achieving your Titan goals, you will feel encouraged to try even harder! In addition, your Victory Logbook will especially come in handy next time you go through a tough time – like everyone does sometimes – when you start losing your confidence or letting your "loser" side come out. In these cases, read your Victory Logbook to remind yourself of the Titan you are!

Whether you are trying to write a book, produce a high-quality product or overcome any life challenges, celebrating your progress, even if small, can make all the difference!

Here are some benefits of keeping a Victory Logbook:

- Boosts **positive emotions and motivation.**
- Increases **confidence.**
- Builds **momentum.**
- Increases **creativity and productivity.**
- Boosts **happiness.**
- Helps you **stay on track** with your goals.
- **Saves your life** when things are looking gloomy.

T

TITAN RECOVERY

*"Our energies are destroyed because of the high tempo,
the abnormal pace at which we go."*
— Norman Vincent Peale

Titans understand the importance of working smart rather than working hard. They know that *Titan Action without Titan Recovery leads to the depletion of the very personal assets that make them a Titan.*

Often, when we think of taking Titan Action toward our goals, we focus only on the performance part, without realizing that the recovery part is equally important.

A Titan Recovery is perhaps the most commonly overlooked aspect of most achievers. Perhaps it's because most achievers feel they're not working hard enough, so the need for rest seems counterintuitive. They're more concerned about underperforming than overperforming.

Did you ever wonder why even though you're eating healthy and are exercising, you're still getting sick? Because when you just focus on the performance part and don't take care of the recovery part, this weakens your immune system, which makes you more susceptible to germs, especially during the flu season.

What's the point of constantly taking action if you then have to call in sick or be at your 50 percent? For building your Titan Life, you cannot afford to be sick or be at your 50 percent!

This is why adding recovery time is essential for health, peak performance and continued progression. Without recovering properly, you will stall your progress – or worse yet, reverse it! Besides, your body is wiser than you. Either you slow down or it will slow you down!

Stress Is Not The Enemy.

"Stress is not necessarily something bad – it all depends on how you take it. The stress of exhilarating, creative successful work is beneficial, while that of failure, humiliation or infection is detrimental."

– Hans Selye

Stress is not the enemy. What's dangerous is not having any recovery period from stress.

There are two types of stress:

1. **Distress** (negative stress). This type of stress is the major cause of most health problems in the world. Stress hormones basically shuts down your life by shutting off your immune system, shutting your growth and triggering reflexive behavior. Pharmaceutical companies love this type of stress, as it creates more profits for them!

2. **Eustress** (positive stress). This type of stress is good for you! It provokes you to perform at your peak, to amp up your game. It works as a stimulus for growth and expansion, so you leave your comfort zone. It pushes you to the edges of your limits.

The key to a Titan Life is not to aim for a zero-stress life, but to *reduce the amount of distress you allow in your life and to recover from the eustress you constantly put yourself through to grow.*

How To Recover Like A Titan.

"Rest is not idleness, and to lie sometimes on the grass under
trees on a summer's day, listening to the murmur of the water,
or watching the clouds float across the sky, is by no
means a waste of time."

– John Lubbock

Recovery does not just take care of itself. It should be a planned element of any Titan.

Titans, even when resting or having a good time, do so to give their mind, body and spirit a break, so they can get back to being Titan with their energies renewed.

To see results from your Titan Action, you must give your mind, body and spirit time to adapt and recover. *Growth, whether mentally, physically or spiritually, does not happen when you actually take action. Instead, it occurs while you recover.*

For a Titan, recovering doesn't mean lounging on the couch all day long, doing nothing. Quite the contrary! A Titan Recovery means *actively* recovering.

The benefit of a Titan Recovery – versus lounging on the couch for hours – is that it'll keep your ideas, blood and spirit flowing! Here are some Titan recovery strategies:

Mental Recovery Strategies.

"Your fishing hours should be as
sacred as your business hours."

– Lin Yutang

- **Read** books daily.
- **Exercise**, at least, 5 days a week for at least 20-30 minutes each time.
- **Practice a hobby,** at least once a week.

- **Take a technology break** at least once a week. Be unreachable!
- **Discard the plan** when you feel like it, but go back to it the next day.
- **Leave your mobile phone out of the bathroom!** Not only will the germs from the toilet and surrounding surfaces get onto your hand and end up on your phone, but also you need peace and quiet for this activity!

Physical Recovery Strategies.

"Recovery is more important to me than actual training sessions due to the large number of games I have to play. Winding down and resting is a key part of my day-to-day routine and enables me to perform to the highest level in my profession and prolong my career."
– Cristiano Ronaldo

- **Low-intensity or de-load workouts.** Easy sessions at no more than 60 to 70 percent of your maximum effort. Do this in the 4th week of each month.
- **Do some yoga or stretching** at least once a week.
- **Sauna or steam room** at least once a week.
- **Low-intensity swimming**. Easy sessions 60 to 70 percent of your maximum effort.
- **Contrast bath therapy**. Alternate cold water (10-15°C or 50-59°F) and hot water (38-40°C or 100-104 °F) immersions for 1-5 minutes each for a 20-30 minute period at least once a week.
- **Get a massage** once a week.
- **Recovery nutrition.**
- **Get adequate sleep** at night and take a nap in the afternoon.

Spiritual Recovery Strategies.

"It does good also to take walks out of doors, that our spirits may be raised and refreshed by the open air and fresh breeze: sometimes we gain strength by driving in a carriage, by travel, by change of air, or by social meals and a more generous allowance of wine."

— *Seneca*

- **Spend time in solitude** to reflect or journal daily.
- **Take a walk** daily.
- Write three things **you are grateful for** daily.
- **Bask in the sun** daily. Around 9:00 AM is the best time for this!
- **Keep human!** Get out of the house, see people, spend time with family & friends.
- **Walk barefoot** on the grass or beach daily, if you can.
- **Watch sunsets daily.** Perhaps even have a light dinner while you do so.
- **Spend time in nature** at least once a week.
- **Treat yourself:** book a room at a fancy hotel, go to a wonderful restaurant, get tickets to the opera, theater or concert, go to a museum, buy some beautiful flowers.
- **Travel** to new places at least once every three months.

Work in Cycles.

"When he worked, he really worked. But when he played, he really played."

— *Dr. Seuss*

You should know by now that working 24x7 will deplete your energy.

Titans, like professional athletes, alternate short cycles of intense performance with cycles of recovery. Both cycles are equally important and necessary, not only to survive but also to thrive!

Titans work more than average, but also rest more than average. Remember this, and you'll be well on your way to becoming a Titan!

Do like professional athletes. Balance your game day with periods of rest.

To know exactly how much work and how much recovery is often a difficult judgment call. You will have to try what works better for you. Here are some Titan strategies:

- **Work 25-5.** Work for 25 minutes and take a 5-minute break (breathe, walk, have a glass of water.)
- **Work 50-10.** Work for 50 minutes and take a 10-minute break (breathe, walk, have a glass of water.)
- **Work 90-20.** Work for 90 minutes and take a 20-minute break (work out, longer walk, have a snack.)
- **Take your lunch hour.** Savor your food. Don't just gulp it down. Sure, sometimes we must rush through our lunch hour, but don't make rushing your normal.
- Take a **20-minute nap** or a **20-minute walk** after lunch. You'll be ready to start all over again! (more on this in a later chapter!)
- **Savor your dinner.** Make it a form of meditation, if alone. Enjoy the conversations, if shared with loved ones. Whether alone or with loved ones, please don't watch TV while eating. Especially, do not watch the news. All those wars and tragedies will not help you with digestion!

- **Take a Titan Rest Day** once a week, where you simply do nothing work-related. Remember, this doesn't mean lounging on the couch!
- **Work for 3 weeks**, take a weekend off.
- **Work for 3 months**, take a week off.
- **Sojourn** in a different city or country for three months every 1 or 2 years.

Relax!

"Tension is who you think you should be.
Relaxation is who you are."
– Chinese proverb

Taking the time to unplug and recharge is critical for our mental, physical, spiritual and emotional well-being.

Many Titans throughout history have used relaxation to boost their happiness, creativity, productivity and overall health: Johann Wolfgang von Goethe, Ludwig van Beethoven, Charles Darwin, Charles Dickens, Nelson Mandela, Warren Buffett, Larry Ellison, Meryl Streep, Richard Branson, Oprah Winfrey, Steve Jobs, Bill Gates, Jeff Bezos and Elon Musk.

Thomas Jefferson said, *"Leave all the afternoon for exercise and recreation, which are as necessary as reading. I will rather say more necessary because health is worth more than learning."*

William S. Burroughs stated, *"Your mind will answer most questions if you learn to relax and wait for the answer."*

And Jeff Bezos stated, *"I like to putter in the morning, so I like to read the newspaper, have coffee, have breakfast with my kids before they go to school. My puttering time is very important for me."*

Here are some of the benefits of relaxing:

- **Reduces stress**, anxiety and depression.
- Improves **overall health.**
- Increases **productivity and creativity.**
- Boosts **happiness.**
- Improves **communication** (walking meetings).

Take A Day Off Weekly.

"Take rest; a field that has rested gives a bountiful crop."
– Ovid

All major religions encourage it! Taking a rest day per week will provide you with a much-needed respite.

Culturally speaking, Jewish people take the concept of rest very seriously. *Sabbath* comes every week, and religious Jews literally stop working for 24 hours, sundown to sundown. They do it for religious reasons, but studies have shown that *taking a day off weekly is Titan for your health and productivity.*

Eckhart Tolle said, *"... the simple reason why the majority of scientists are not creative is not because they don't know how to think, but because they don't know how to stop thinking!"*

So if you want to be a Titan, take at least a day off each week!

Here are some of its benefits:

- **Reduces negative stress** and allow you to recover from positive stress you constantly push yourself through.
- **Reduces inflammation** and the risk of heart disease.
- **Boosts your immune system**.

- **Restores** physical, mental and spiritual energies.
- Brings the opportunity to **connect with your loved ones**.

Titan Recreation.

*"I don't think of work as work and
play as play. It's all living."*
– *Richard Branson*

Titans know of the importance of Titan recreation to have a Titan Life.

Oprah Winfrey likes gardening; Richard Branson plays chess; Bill Gates and Warren Buffet play bridge (Buffett also plays the ukulele); Larry Ellison likes sailing; Meryl Streep likes knitting.

Don't wait to have fun or travel until you retire. Celebrate life while you climb to the mountain top!

Build a system to ensure that each week you have some adventure and fun. Make time for Titan recreation: practice a hobby, go see a movie, get a massage, go to your favorite bookstore, read an interesting book, go to new places, try some new food, learn a new skill, go to a museum. Be a kid again!

Human life goes in cycles of work and play, of tension and relaxation. As Miguel de Cervantes wrote, *"The bow cannot always stand bent, nor can human frailty subsist without some lawful recreation."*

What's the point of realizing your Titan goals if you haven't had time to have fun? Life is a giant adventure. Enjoy it! The person who experiences the most wins! At the end of your life, it won't be the Rolls-Royces, but the experiences that will stay with you.

Take Vacations. Really!

"When you go on vacation, your routine is interrupted;
the places you go and the new people you meet can
inspire you in unexpected ways."

– Richard Branson

Most people are not growing because their brain is suffering from over-stimulation.

Research has proven that long periods of work without vacation can lead to reduced productivity, diminished creativity and strained relationships.

Contrary to popular belief, Titans take time off.

Williams James said, *"Every man who possibly can should force himself to a holiday of a full month in a year, whether he feels like taking it or not."*

Richard Branson said, *"I make sure that I disconnect by leaving my smartphone at home or in the hotel room for as long as possible – days, if I can – and bringing a notepad and pen with me instead. Freed from the daily stresses of my working life, I find that I am more likely to have new insights into old problems and other flashes of inspiration."*

And Red Hastings, who publicly announced that he takes six weeks of vacation a year because "it's important for work-life balance," said, *"It is helpful. You often do your best thinking when you're off hiking in some mountain or something. You get a different perspective on things."*

Don't wait for retirement to take some time off! Aim to distribute mini-retirements throughout life. You not only need time to recover and bond with your family, but also you will get your Titan ideas about your professional and personal lives while you are vacationing.

Did you finish your Titan project? Celebrate with your family! Take them on a trip!

Travel.

"He who returns from a journey
is not the same as he who left."

      – Chinese Proverb

Traveling is one of the secrets to becoming a Titan.

Many Titans throughout history have used traveling to disrupt who they were yesterday.

Socrates stated, *"I'm from the world; not from Athens."*

Augustine of Hippo said, *"The world is a book, and those who don't travel only read one page."*

Seneca stated, "Travel and change of place impart new vigor to the mind."

And Dalai Lama said, *"Once a year, go someplace you've never been before."*

By exposing yourself to different cultures, different foods and different ways of operating, you will realize that no country by itself has all the answers. There is no perfect country out there! Every country has some Titan aspects – and some not so Titan. *By embracing all the Titan aspects from all different cultures around the world, you get to form your own culture back home.*

Feel as comfortable in Tokyo, Delhi and Madrid, as you feel back home. Meet new interesting people, new cultures, new foods. Become a citizen of the world! Realize that we are all connected by our humanity.

Don't wait to travel until you retire! Do it now, while you're still young! If you are concerned about the cost of traveling, know that *traveling is the only thing you buy that makes you richer*. Try backpacking, instead!

When you travel, your perspective is altered, so that you see the world through someone else's eyes. This is called *empathy*. And with more empathy in the world, we would solve most of today's world problems.

T

TITAN SPIRIT

*"Being spiritual has nothing to do with what you believe and
everything to do with your state of consciousness."*
— Eckhart Tolle

Many people, especially in the more economically
developed countries, have become obsessed with developing
the mind. While developing the mind is also important,
everything starts with developing the spirit.

The spirit is wiser than the mind. While your mind offers
knowledge, your spirit offers wisdom.

The spirit is the master of your entire being. The spirit has
been described as the king, with the mind as the king's
adviser. When faced with a difficult decision, the king may
ask his adviser for advice. It may even send him out into the
world to gather facts, but ultimately it is the king that must
make the final decision. The king is always right because he
sees the whole picture from a higher place.

The problem is that most people follow their minds —
instead of their spirits — believing it will solve all of their
life's problems. This is not the right approach!

While the mind can understand the most complex
scientific and mathematical theories, the mind can also get
caught up in trivia and nonsense. Your mind contains all
your wounds and fears. This is why, if your mind dominates
your life, you will be at its mercy, and it will push and pull
you in all directions, creating problems and dramas. Your

spirit has no wounds and knows nothing of fear. Your spirit is innocent, utterly blissful!

If you're not sure about the above statement, why is it that you, my mind-developed friend, are not happy?

While you might think there are numerous reasons you are not happy, the main reason is that your mind is not standing in the proper position. Your mind has surpassed the spirit and, having reversed the order, has risen from the position of an advisor to becoming the king. And this is when you're in trouble! Because living inside your head all the time is not conducive to your happiness!

So what is the spirit? The spirit is your *awareness*.

Most of the world's problems, including your own – whether it is your health, marriage, family, finances – are due to a lack of awareness. As Lao Tzu said, *"The key to growth is the introduction of higher dimensions of consciousness into our awareness."*

And when you develop awareness about yourself, you can also develop awareness about others. And this, my friend, is called *empathy*!

You Are Not Your Thoughts.

"What a liberation to realize that the "voice in my head" is not who I am. Who am I then? The one who sees that."
– Eckhart Tolle

Have you ever thought about killing your boss or hitting someone's car for rudely cutting you off in traffic?

These thoughts might flash into your mind, but then you simply label them as *thoughts* and let them pass like a cloud, without judging or rejecting them. They are just thoughts!

The fact that you can watch your mind's thoughts means *you are not your thoughts; you are above them!*

As the pen is not the writer, but an instrument in the hands of the writer, *the mind is not the master, but an instrument in the hands of the master.* A Titan Life is about having mastery over yourself.

Become The Observer.

"Watch your thoughts, they become your words; watch your words, they become your actions; watch your actions, they become your habits; watch your habits, they become your character; watch your character, it becomes your destiny."
— *Lao Tzu*

Rather than being your thoughts, be the awareness behind them. *Become the observer of your thoughts.*

Thoughts in themselves aren't positive or negative as they enter your mind; they are actually *neutral*. But they can be empowering or disempowering to your happiness and success, depending on the meaning you, the observer, decide to give them. And who is this you? Your awareness, your spirit.

To build your Titan Life, you must stand at the doorway of your mind and monitor your thoughts. Entertain only those thoughts conducive to your Titan Life, and discard those that are not.

Whenever a disempowering thought pops in your mind, say, *"Stop! Thank you for sharing"* (preventing a potential 'snowball effect'). Next, replace that disempowering thought for its empowering counterpart, *even if at the moment it may seem delusional.* Repeat the empowering thought, over and over again, until the disempowering thought goes away.

The quality of your life depends upon the quality of your thoughts, so choose wisely!

Developing Titan Optimism.

"Overcoming negative tendencies and enhancing positive potential are the very essence of the spiritual path."
— Dalai Lama

Stoics – such as Seneca and Epictetus – believed that the objective of the virtuous person is to reach *apatheia* – a state of tranquility: the absence of negative feelings such as anxiety, fear and anger, and the presence of positive feelings such as happiness, love and gratitude.

Your success does not create your optimism. *It is your optimism that leads to your success.*

Titans are optimists. The word "optimism" actually derives from the Latin word *optima*, which means *the best outcome or belief in the greatest good.*

While most people look for ways that something cannot be done, Titans look for ways it can be done. While most people focus on problems, Titans focus on solutions. While most people kill opportunities, Titans create them.

I am not suggesting to pretend that everything is rosy when it is not. But *we can choose to look at things in a way that empowers us.* This way of looking at things is not "true" in an absolute sense, but it is more useful, and feels a lot better!

A Titan optimism is not passive. You don't simply focus on the positives and do nothing about it, hoping that the universe will give you that which you want. A Titan optimism is proactive. You focus on the positive while doing something about it!

Overcoming Crisis.

*"When crisis comes, the first thing I ask is,
'What are you here to teach me?"*

– Oprah Winfrey

One thing is to prevent disempowering thoughts from taking over your mind – this, you can control – and another thing is to prevent a crisis from happening – this, you cannot always control.

Life isn't all about fun and games. We lose our jobs; we get divorced; we get physically injured or sick; a parent dies. These are part of life, and you can't control them from happening. But you can always control one thing, *your reaction!*

While it is important that you feel the pain and grieve (journaling is a Titan tool for this!), you must not dwell on suffering. Like the Dalai Lama says, *"Pain is inevitable. Suffering is optional."*

As painful as it may seem at the moment, always ask yourself, *'What is this here to teach me?'* Whenever you do this, you will find clarity and then a way to better shoulder the burden.

A crisis is only a problem if you make the choice to see it as a problem. The word 'crisis' in Japanese (危機) has the kanjis 危 (danger) and 機 (opportunity). Everyone has crises in life. It is up to us to see a crisis as danger or problem, or as an opportunity for growth!

Your growth can only grow to the extent that you do. The size of the crisis is never the issue. *What matters is the size of you!* If you have a "big" crisis in your life, all it means is that you are being a small person. The bigger the crises you can handle, the bigger the opportunities you will create. And if you become a master at handling crises, what can stop you from success? Nothing! And if nothing can stop you from success, nothing will stop you from living your Titan Life! So always ask yourself, *"What is this here to teach me?"*

Practice "Negative Visualization."

"We should love all our dear ones…, but always with the thought that we have no promise that we may keep them forever – nay, no promise even that we may keep them for long."
– *Seneca*

The thing we love can fall at any moment with a gust of wind. Everything we have and all the people we love disappear at some point.

Stoics practiced *negative visualization*. They imagined the worst thing that could happen to be prepared if certain privileges and pleasures were taken away from them. To practice *negative visualization* correctly, we have to *reflect on negative events, but without worrying about them.*

Seneca not only practiced *negative visualization* every night before falling asleep, but also put it into practice – for example, by living for a week without servants.

Here are some ways you can practice *negative visualization*:

- What if your important event (exam, meeting, work presentation, marriage) were to go wrong? What's the worst possible scenario? What would you do?
- What if a loved one would suddenly die? How would you feel? What would you like to tell them now?
- What if you lost all your possessions now? What would you do?
- What if you died today or get terminally ill? How would this impact your life, your relationships?

Negative visualization works similar to a vaccine as it improves your defense mechanisms when misfortunes happen. This practice will teach you to *appreciate more what you already have without clinging to it, so you will be prepared to let go of the things and people you appreciate no matter what life throws at you.*

Your anticipation of difficult scenarios takes the sting and fear out of them by reducing the surprise factor and by confronting them through your imagination.

Taming Fear.

"I never take counsel of my fears."
– General George Patton

Have you ever been scared? Have you ever felt "butterflies" in your stomach before an important event, date, exam, job interview? Well, join the club! This means you are human.

Fear is a normal human survival mechanism that helped us when we had to fight saber-tooth tigers in the savanna. But fear does not serve us now!

Fear is the primary obstacle you are facing right now that is preventing you from living your Titan Life. Why? Because fear keeps you small!

Here's a Titan secret: *"Everyone, including Titans, experiences fear or anxiety from time to time before an important undertaking. The difference between Titans and most people is that even though they both feel the same "butterflies," the latter let their fear paralyze them, while the former decides to step forward in spite of feeling the same "butterflies." In other words, most people run away from fear, while Titans run towards it!"*

Overcoming fear comes down to the attitude you choose to take: to fight and resist fear – which is not advisable – or to acknowledge and accept fear, and still take a step forward!

Fear is a great teacher. It provides a great source of information and data. It's a sign-post of where you need to grow. The thing that most terrifies you is what you must do because it will bring you the greatest growth.

So get to know your fears. Journal about them. Understand them. Befriend them. Say, *"Alright, so I'm feeling butterflies... my mouth is dry, oh, hi, fear!"* Give a big smile. And now say, *"Fear, thanks for sharing, but I need to move forward!"*

Action dissipates fear. I did not say "eliminates" because fear will always be there. Get used to it! To be human is to deal with fear. Courage is not the absence of fear. *Courage is recognizing your fears and still do whatever needs to be done!* As Mark Twain said, *"Courage is resistance to fear, mastery of fear, not absence of fear."*

What is it you are currently resisting the most? This is what you must do! Are you afraid of heights? Go to the tallest building and look down over the edge! *Constant exposure to the object of fear immunizes against the fear.*

Each time you do what scares you, you take back the power you gave to that very thing you gave your power to. And you will build character. *On the other side of your fear lies your Titan Life.*

The Master and the Dogs.

"One day, a wise Master went to visit a remote mountain temple. As he approached the temple, he saw a pair of ferocious dogs chained to the entry gate. Upon seeing the

Master, the dogs barked and pulled against their chains.
monk accompanying the Master said, 'I know these dog.
look scary but don't worry; they are chained to the wall and
cannot harm you.' As the Master and monk passed the
entrance to the temple, the Master looked back to see that
the dogs had broken free from their chains and were racing
directly towards him. Then, the Master started to run –
directly towards the dogs. The dogs were so surprised to see
the Master running at them that they turned around and ran
away."

Be Comfortable Being Uncomfortable.

"Twenty years from now you will be more disappointed by the
things that you didn't do than by the ones you did do. So throw
off the bowlines. Sail away from the safe harbor. Catch the
trade winds in your sails. Explore. Dream. Discover."

– Mark Twain

Discomfort is the price that Titans pay. Christopher Columbus was the first one to sail perpendicular to the coast, instead of parallel to the coast like the rest did.

If it is not uncomfortable, you are not making progress. To grow as a person, you need to expand your comfort zone. You only grow when you are outside your comfort zone. Whenever you feel uncomfortable, say to yourself, *'I must be growing,'* and continue moving forward! Progress lives in the edges.

It is possible to act independently of or even in opposition to our thoughts and feelings. For example, most professional actors get nervous before getting on the stage. They feel "butterflies," but they still do it! The key is to *step forward, in spite of how you feel.* Acting confidently, even when you

:reates a level of real confidence within that
n."

de your traditional comfort zone of
ires substantial motivation and sacrifice,
y discipline. And as you keep expanding
your comfort zone – through taking action – what used to be
scary, unknown, or extraordinary becomes now the new
comfort zone!

Titan Discipline.

"If I want to be great I have to win the
victory over myself... self-discipline."
– Harry S. Truman

Having an impulse is normal. Making the decision is
optional. Every time you have the discipline not to follow
your human impulse, you are building character.

As the Bible says, *"He that ruleth his spirit is better than*
he that taketh a city."

Here are some simple strategies that will indirectly help
you build Titan Discipline:

- Wake up **early.**
- **Make** your bed.
- **Work out** in the morning.
- **Brush your teeth** every morning and every evening.
- **Leave a portion of your favorite dessert or treat.**
  You're telling your brain – and life – who's boss!
- **Floss your teeth** in the evening.
- Go to bed **early.**

Developing Titan Faith.

"Faith is taking the first step even when
you don't see the whole staircase."
– Martin Luther King Jr.

Faith is a product of the spirit, not the mind. In fact, the mind will interfere in the process of faith more than it contributes to it. *So to have faith even when things are going bad will require us to quiet the mind.*

The word faith in Greek is *pistis*, which means confidence or trust. Faith is seeing with your eyes closed. *It is knowing – even though you don't know – that things will unfold exactly the way you know they will.* It is trusting beyond all reason and evidence you will come out victorious. *The only times that faith will not work is when you, deep inside, think that you are not good enough to receive that which you say you want.*

Do not think of it as in religious faith, although they work the same. In fact, Dr. Alexis Carrel, in writing of his personal observations of instantaneous healings at Lourdes, France, said that the only explanation he could make as a medical doctor was that the body's own natural healing process, which normally operate over time to bring about healing, were somehow "speeded up" under the influence of intense faith.

Can you imagine how Titan you would become if you developed the same type of "intense faith" in yourself?

As Napoleon Hill said, *"Faith and fear make poor bedfellows. Where one is found, the other cannot exist."*

Becoming More Aware.

"Awareness is like the sun.
When it shines on things, they are transformed."
– Thich Nhat Hanh

We know by now that the more aware we become, the better our lives will be.

So the question is, *How do we become more aware of the different aspects of our life?* In other words, how do we achieve mastery over ourselves, so we can choose our thoughts and actions?

Here's a secret that all Titans throughout history have used: *spend time in silence and solitude.* Your life will be transformed!

Silence and Solitude.

"Your soul needs time for solitude and self-reflection. In order
to love, lead, heal, and create, you must nourish yourself first."
– Louise Hay

Silence and solitude have been used by Titans throughout history to *get guidance from within*: Buddha, Jesus, Muhammad, Plato, Marcus Aurelius, Seneca, Montaigne, Goethe, Lincoln, Emerson, Thoreau, Theodore Roosevelt, Winston Churchill, and Mother Teresa all practiced silence and solitude.

May Sarton said, *"Solitude is the richness of self."*

Baltasar Gracián *stated, "Self-reflection is the school of wisdom."*

And Santiago Ramón y Cajal said, *"Oh comforting solitude, how favorable thou art to original thought!"*

In our crowded, noisy, modern world, silence and solitude seem out of reach to the average man. It seems reserved only for the religious ascetics or the billionaires who can afford it. Yet, to build a Titan Life, *you cannot afford not to spend time in silence and solitude!*

Titans carve out some solitude time daily to gain awareness about the different aspects of their lives.

Your inner voice, your true self, your breakthrough ideas all live in the room of silence and solitude.

You have only to wake up twenty to thirty minutes before the rest of your family does. Yes, any time of the day will be well spent in silence and solitude, but there is something magical about doing it upon rising in the morning. Note: no electronic devices, please!

So what do you do during this time of silence and solitude? While sitting still and spending time in silence and solitude is a discipline in itself, here are some Titan strategies you might want to include:

- Journaling.
- Gratitude.

Journaling.

"The unexamined life is not worth living."

– Socrates

Journaling is another great tool that many Titans have used throughout history: Albert Einstein, Marie Curie, Mark Twain, Charles Darwin, Thomas Alva Edison, Frida Kahlo and Leonardo Da Vinci all kept journals.

Maya Angelou said, *"I've always written [on journals]. There's a journal which I kept from about 9 years old."*

Martina Navratilova stated, *"Keeping a journal of what's going on in your life is a good way to help you distill what's important and what's not."*

And Jim Rohn said, *"If you're serious about becoming a wealthy, powerful, sophisticated, healthy, influential, cultured, and unique individual, keep a journal. Keeping a journal is so important. I call it one of the three treasures to leave behind for the next generation..."*

Journaling to develop a Titan Spirit is not about writing perfectly, sounding smart or even being grammatically correct. Journaling is about *having a conversation with yourself.* So you get to know yourself, your talents, what you stand for, what you want your life to become, what's most important to you. So every area of your life becomes clear and you become aware of what needs to be improved.

When you journal, you start noticing patterns. And, once you are aware of certain patterns, it is very difficult to complain about a situation morning after morning, week after week, without being moved to constructive action!

When it comes to journaling, handwriting wins over typing. While typing on the keyboard encourages verbatim notes without giving much thought to the information, handwriting forces your brain to mentally engage with the information, improving reading comprehension and allowing short- and long-term memory recall.

Here are some of the benefits of keeping a journal:

- **Helps bridge and integrate your conscious and subconscious minds**. While any time you carve out time for journaling is time well spent, *the best time to access your subconscious mind is journaling upon rising*. This is the time when your most genuine thoughts and your "darkest secrets" you've been hiding from yourself come out.

- **Multiplies your clarity.** Journaling is a way of thinking. It clarifies thought and helps break the whole into its parts. This way, you can plan out your options and consider multiple outcomes of a situation. As Napoleon Hill said, *"If you don't know why you failed, you are no wiser than when you began."*

- **Releases your repressed and suppressed emotions, including stress and anxiety.** Journaling forces you to "search your feelings." *Journaling is, without a doubt, your best shrink.* It helps us detect sneaky, unhealthy patterns in our thoughts and behaviors, allowing us to take more control over our lives and put things in perspective. So next time something hurts or makes you anxious, put it down on paper! Did you have a bad day at work? Put it down on paper before you put it on your family! *Titan note: If you want no one to read what you wrote, you can throw away the pages!

- **Propels you toward your goals.** By writing down your goals and keeping track of your progress, it will help you bring your Titan Vision to life.

- **Deepens understanding.** If you don't learn from your mistakes, you are doomed to repeat them! Reflect on them, figure out what went wrong and see how we can prevent this from happening again.

- **Brings perspective.** Often, we are caught up in the troubles or busy-ness of our daily lives. However, if we take a minute to step back and reflect on these problems, we realize how in the grand scheme of things, they don't mean that much.

- **Records your Titan Life** (trips, events, conversations, meals.) Take pictures of your life and paste them on your journal, and write about those moments. Journaling leaves a written record of your experiences, which can be helpful today and extremely precious in the future.

- **Improves your creativity.** While your left side of the brain is occupied, your right side – the creative side – is given the freedom to wander and play. Allowing your creativity to flourish can make a Titan difference in your daily well-being.
- **Boosts your happiness.** It helps us shift from a negative mindset to a more positive one. Thus, it improves your relationships with others!
- **Makes you healthier.** Strengthens your immune system, drops your blood pressure and helps you sleep better.
- **Helps you discover your "voice."**

Gratitude.

"When you arise in the morning, think of what a precious privilege it is to be alive - to breathe, to think, to enjoy, to love."

– Marcus Aurelius

Gratitude is the antidote to fear. Gratitude is the antidote to unhappiness. You can't be fearful and grateful at the same time. You can't be unhappy and grateful at the same time. You are fearless and happy because you are grateful. Not the other way around!

Gratitude is powerful because it shifts your focus. Life is all about focus. Whatever you focus on, you move towards. When you focus on all the things wrong with your life, guess what you attract more of (without mentioning the energy and time you wasted!) When you focus on all the blessings in your life, you move from living in a state of lack to living in a state of abundance. And the more you live in a state of abundance, the more abundance you will manifest. Put in a different way, *gratitude always preludes the attainment of Titan things in life!*

As Oprah Winfrey said, *"I live in the space of thankfulness – and I have been rewarded a million times over for it. I started out giving thanks for small things, and the more thankful I became, the more my bounty increased. That's because what you focus on expands, and when you focus on the goodness in your life, you create more of it. Opportunities, relationships, even money flowed my way when I learned to be grateful no matter what happened in my life."*

Cultivating gratitude has been shown to be an extremely effective tool for improving the quality of our life and reaching our goals.

Here are some benefits of being grateful:

- **Reduces stress**, depression and anxiety.
- Improves **self-awareness.**
- Enhances **resilience.**
- **Lowers fatigue** and depression.
- Improves **sleep.**
- Improves **social interactions.**

So remember to be grateful daily, not just on Thanksgiving! You can't think of anything to be grateful for? How about the *opportunity to be alive, to breathe*?

T

TITAN MIND

"The mind is everything. What you think you become."
– Buddha

Is your mind preventing you from living your Titan Life? Chances are good that it is. Here's why:

Primarily, the human mind protects you to ensure your survival, safety and security. This process is almost certainly linked to our ancient survival mechanisms from our pre-human days, millions of years ago, when we had to fight wild animals!

So if the primary purpose of your mind is to keep you safe, do you think that your mind's natural tendency is to help you become successful and live your Titan Life, which implies taking risks and leaving your comfort zone? You guessed right!

Titans are aware of the importance of developing a Titan Mind in order to live a Titan Life.

As Ralph Waldo Emerson said, *"Sow a thought and you reap an action; sow an act and you reap a habit; sow a habit and you reap a character; sow a character and you reap a destiny."*

Understanding The Mind.

"The mind is like an iceberg, it floats
with one-seventh of its bulk above water."
– Sigmund Freud

We have two minds, or if you prefer, two parts to one mind: the conscious mind and the subconscious mind.

The **conscious mind** is our *thinking* mind. It contains the thoughts, memories, feelings, and wishes of which we are aware. This is the aspect of our mental processing we can think and talk about rationally.

The **subconscious mind** is the part of the mind not currently in focal awareness, but contains the data of all programmed behaviors (both by the person's unique genetic inheritance – *inborn* – and by the person's social conditioning – *learned*.) The subconscious mind's mission is *to ensure that you respond exactly the way you are programmed.* There is no thinking in these subconscious behaviors. In the words of Dr. Bruce Lipton, *"it's more like push-the-button, play-the-program."* So everything you say and do fit a pattern consistent with your programming.

Here's the interesting thing: *95% – 99% of the decisions you make daily are made by your subconscious mind. Meaning, you don't even know why you are making them.* If the conscious mind represents the tip of the iceberg, it is the subconscious mind that makes up the massive bulk that lies beneath.

Early Programming Will Determine Your Destiny… If You Let It!

"Give me the child until it is seven years old and I will give you the man."
– Ignatius of Loyola

A man's destiny is shaped from the last trimester of pregnancy through the first seven years of a child's life… if you let it!

You learn most of your programmed behaviors at a young age. They are derived from recording the behaviors of those around you: your parents, siblings, teachers, friends, society. *The world around you shapes the way you think.* It's sort of like an unconscious hypnosis.

Most people go through life with the programming instilled in them at a young age. This is why children of doctors become doctors, why children of soccer players become soccer players or why children of alcoholics end up marrying alcoholic spouses.

If you were born in a family with a Titan programming, the chances of you becoming a Titan immediately increase. Conversely, if you were born in a family with non-successful programming, the chances of you becoming non-successful also immediately increase. This is why most people are "victims of their unlucky circumstances," without realizing that they could, borrowing Dr. John Demartini's words, *"become the master of their destiny and not the victim of their history."*

Your destiny has been shaped during the first seven years of your life, *unless* you do something about it.

Your Subconscious Mind Runs Your Life.

"If you do not run your subconscious mind yourself, someone else will run it for you."
– Florence Scovel Shinn

Your subconscious mind is a creature of habit. It thrives upon the dominating thoughts fed.

You may "say" that you want to be a professional basketball player, but do you think about becoming a professional basketball player most of the time? Or do you think about girls and video games most of the time?

You don't get that which you "say" you want, but that which you subconsciously want.

We all have goals, whether we intentionally articulate them or not. Our subconscious mind is continually leading us toward the images we have stored in our subconscious mind. For instance, the alcoholic or drug addict has goals just as much as the entrepreneur, professional athlete, or writer.

The subconscious mind cannot move outside its planted programs. It automatically reacts to situations with its stored behavior responses, and it works without the knowledge or control of the conscious mind. This is why we are generally unaware of our behavior. Most of the time we are not even aware that we are acting subconsciously.

With this in mind, we can become aware of what's "under the hood," and whether or not we want the goals we're subconsciously moving toward, or the ones that we consciously choose and work toward.

As Epictetus said, *"If you yourself don't choose what thoughts and images you expose yourself to, someone else will."*

How You See The World.

"Everything we hear is an opinion, not a fact.
Everything we see is a perspective, not the truth."
– Marcus Aurelius

We see the world, not as it is, but as we are – or, as we have been conditioned or programmed to see it.

Each one of us has a personal lens through which we see how the world operates. This personal lens was shaped by our well-intentioned parents, our teachers, our friends, the society we live in. For instance, if your father feared taking risks, there is a good chance that you are now also afraid of taking risks. If your teachers – or at least the ones that affected you the most – taught you that pursuing a college degree was more important than pursuing your dreams, there is a good chance that you now think the same. If your friends used to make fun of gay people, there is a good chance that now you are also making fun of gay people. And if the society you were raised in classified humans in different racial groups, there is a good chance that you now also see the world in racial groups.

Your truths are your subconscious beliefs. And your subconscious beliefs are simply the "stories" that you have been passed on – or that *you have rehearsed enough times* until they became part of your subconscious mind – and accepted as "truths."

We, humans, are always congruent with our subconscious beliefs. The areas of your life that are working reflect the subconscious beliefs in your mind that are working. The areas of your life not working reflect the subconscious beliefs in your mind not working. This is why *you will never rise any higher than your subconscious beliefs.*

Here's the good news: You can reshape the lens through which you see the world! As Lao Tzu said, *"When I let go of what I am, I become what I might be."*

Neuroplasticity.

"Any man could, if he were so inclined,
be the sculptor of his own brain."
– Santiago Ramon y Cajal

Neuroplasticity is the ability of the brain to form new connections and pathways and change how its circuits are wired. In simple terms, *your brain is like a muscle you can develop, sculpt and grow.*

This idea is not a new concept. It goes back to the early 1900s when Santiago Ramón y Cajal, the "father of neuroscience," talked about *neuronal plasticity.* He recognized that, in contrast to the belief at that time, brains could change after a person had reached adulthood.

The brain you are born with is not the brain you are stuck with for life. Your brain, like any other muscle, can be exercised. As you can grow your biceps with work, you can also grow your IQ with work. This confirms that you don't have the brain you want. You have the brain you earn!

Reprogram Your Subconscious Mind.

"Whatever we plant in our subconscious mind and nourish with repetition and emotion will one day become a reality."
– Earl Nightingale

Belief is a product of the mind. And if it is a product of the mind, you can change it. Therefore, *you can change your beliefs*!

To change a belief that no longer serves you, you must change your subconscious programming. And to change your subconscious programming, *you must work on it through conscious repetition.*

As you can train a dog with repetition, you can train your subconscious mind to accept and adopt a new idea. You can consciously release any thought or belief that is not supportive of your health, wealth and happiness, and replace it for one that is.

Stop the old stories you have been telling yourself. You can rewrite any program in your life. And when you change your story, your performance will match your new belief. There is really no magic here, except for the *magic of the human brain*!

Here are some Titan strategies that will help you reprogram your subconscious mind:

- Affirmations.
- Visualization.
- Reading.

In the same way that you do reps at the gym to improve your body, *affirmations, visualization and reading are exercises to improve your mind and outlook on life*. These positive mental reps help you reprogram your thinking patterns so that, over time, you think – and act – differently.

Affirmations.

"You affect your subconscious mind by verbal repetition."
– W. Clement Stone

Affirmations are positive statements that can help you reprogram your mind, *when repeated often, and when you believe in them*.

You must be careful about the affirmations you – consciously or unconsciously – choose because, whether positive or negative, *your brain does not differentiate and will believe it*. You attract what you constantly tell yourself. So if you constantly tell yourself the wrong thing, you will produce the wrong thing!

Have you ever said to yourself, *"I'm so dumb"* after making a small mistake? Tell yourself this often enough, and you will become a true dummy!

We all sometimes have negative self-talk. Replace this by its positive counterpart. For example, replace *"I can't* finish writing this book" by *"I will* finish writing this book!"

Titans never say, *"I'm so dumb"* or *"my memory is not good enough"* or *"I'm not good at public speaking"* or *"that would never work"* or *"that's impossible."*

The words you use have power over your brain. Use the language of Titans versus the vocabulary of a victim. There isn't such a thing as a "Titan victim." Don't make excuses. Behind every excuse, there is always fear. Stop complaining. Don't give away your power. Don't focus on limitations. You strengthen what you speak about. If you complain or make up excuses, you will believe it. Words have power. Speak like a Titan. Titans are impeccable with their words.

Maxwell Maltz wrote, *"It is no exaggeration to say that every human being is hypnotized to some extent either by ideas he has uncritically accepted from others or ideas he has repeated to himself or convinced himself are true."*

Use affirmations to persuade your subconscious mind you can do anything you wish! An affirmation must be *positive, personal, present tense (or present continuous), visual and emotional.* Repeat your affirmations several times a day until it becomes an automatic response whenever you doubt yourself.

As a self-fulfilling prophecy is a prediction that directly or indirectly causes itself to become true by the very terms of the prophecy itself, *an affirmation, when repeated, even if it is actually false, it will eventually cause itself to become true.* We come to believe anything we tell ourselves often enough, even if it is not true!

As Lady Gaga said, *"It's sorta like a mantra. You repeat it to yourself every day. 'Music is my life, music is my life. The fame is inside of me, I'm going to make a number one record with number one hits.' And it's not yet, it's a lie. You're saying a lie over and over again and one day the lie is true."*

Here are some examples of affirmations:

- I'm the best player in the world.
- I'm writing a best-selling book.
- I speak confidently.

Visualization.

"Visualize this thing that you want. See it, feel it, believe in it. Make your mental blueprint, and begin to build."

– Robert Collier

We become or attract into our lives that which we visualize or think about most of the time.

In neuroscience, a number of experiments have shown that people can actually change their brain structure – regardless of their age! – by creating new neural pathways just *by conscious thinking.*

The brain does not differentiate between a real memory and an imagined or visualized one. This means that *when you imagine something vividly and with emotion, your brain chemistry changes as though the experience had actually happened, and your mind records it as a real memory.* Because of this characteristic of the mind, you can use visualization to build self-confidence, develop new skills faster and achieve your goals.

Titans use visualization. Before a performance, a difficult confrontation, or the daily challenge of meeting a goal,

Titans "see" it, feel it and experience it, repeatedly, before they actually do it. *They visualize not only the desired end result but also all the necessary steps to make it happen.* They create an internal "comfort zone," so when they get in the situation, it isn't foreign. It doesn't scare them!

Visualization communicates what to focus on to the mind. It's important that you tell your mind what to focus on because *the object of your focus determines your perception of reality.*

If you want your mind to work to your advantage – at noticing opportunities that will take you closer to your objectives – you must program it by visualizing your goals. Visualization will give you the energy to move forward!

Napoleon Bonaparte practiced soldiering in his imagination for many years before he ever went on an actual battlefield.

Albert Einstein said, *"Everything is energy and that's all there is to it. Match the frequency of the reality you want and you cannot help but get that reality. It can be no other way. This is not philosophy. This is physics."*

Dr. Norman Vincent Peale wrote, *"Formulate and stamp indelibly on your mind a mental picture of yourself as succeeding. Hold this picture tenaciously and never permit it to fade. Your mind will seek to develop this picture!"*

And Michael Jordan said, *"Every time I feel tired while exercising and training, I close my eyes to see that picture, to see that list with my name. This usually motivates me to work again."*

How to Properly Do Affirmations and Visualization.

"Conscious auto-suggestion, made with confidence, faith, and
perseverance realizes itself automatically,
in all matters within reason."

– Émile Coué

The best time to practice affirmations and visualization is as you wake up. Without getting into the scientific explanation, *the first 20-30 minutes after waking up is the time your subconscious mind is more impressionable, and it is easier for you to reprogram patterns and beliefs at a subconscious level.* Affirmations and visualization under this deep level of relaxation are also known as *self-hypnosis.*

Whatever you hear, see or are exposed to in that first 20-30 minute window will affect you and set the tone for the rest of your day.

If every morning, upon rising, you visualize yourself accomplishing something while at these levels of the mind, you will override your old, limiting beliefs that have prevented you from succeeding in the past with a new belief: *your capacity to achieve it!*

How to properly practice affirmations and visualization is relatively simple, but there are definitely a few steps to follow to make it effective and bring the desired results:

1. **Close your eyes and take a deep breath**. It's important to be as relaxed as possible.

2. **Think about a past victory, even if it is a small one.** To direct your brain toward success, instead of failure, all you need is *one experience* that made you feel good about yourself in the past. It could be as simple as learning how to tie your shoes or passing that "big" test in elementary school. This one positive memory, no matter how small or long ago it

took place, is all you need to recapture "that winning feeling."

3. **Say your Affirmation.** Say what you want to achieve – your desired end result. Set your intention. Be as clear with the universe as possible! You may repeat this affirmation as often as you find necessary *to help you transition into the realm of the imagination.*

4. **Imagine the situation or future event you would like to achieve.** Make the scene as real as you can, like a simulation, using your five senses. The more vividly you can imagine the scene, the better it will be recorded in your mind as a "real memory." Always incorporate strong positive emotions. This is key! *Without a strong emotion, the event visualized won't seem real enough to be recorded as a memory.*

5. **Repeat this ritual often.** Do this every morning until you notice desirable changes in your behavior, skills, confidence, etc.

Other Forms Of Affirmations And Visualization.

- **Prayer.** It has the same positive effects as long as the prayer is *personal, positive, present tense (or present continuous), visual and emotional,* and as long as you pray with the belief – faith – that the outcome will come true.
- **Titan Vision Board.** Get images of your Titan Life cut out from magazines or printed from the internet. Put them up in your bathroom mirror or in front of your treadmill at home. Look at them every morning. This will remind you of your intent: *How could I make it happen?*

Reading.

"Nurture your minds with great thoughts.
To believe in the heroic makes heroes."

– Benjamin Disraeli

Titans are curious people with a voracious appetite for reading and learning. Here is a list of Titans who were – or are – avid readers: Alexander the Great, Leonardo Da Vinci, Benjamin Franklin, Abraham Lincoln, Ralph Waldo Emerson, Mark Twain, Thomas Alva Edison, Nikola Tesla, Theodore Roosevelt, the Wright Brothers, Mahatma Gandhi, Winston Churchill, Albert Einstein, Ernest Hemingway, Jorge Luis Borges, José Saramago, Martin Luther King Jr., Warren Buffet, Bruce Springsteen, Oprah Winfrey, Steve Jobs, Bill Gates, Barack Obama, the list goes on.

Philosopher Epictetus stated, *"Books are the training weights of the mind."*

Abraham Lincoln said, *"A capacity, and taste, for reading gives access to whatever has already been discovered by others."*

Charlie Munger stated, *"Without lifelong* learning*, you're not going to do very well. You're not going to get very far in life based on what you already know."*

And Bill Gates said, *"Every book teaches me something new or helps me see things differently."*

The person who doesn't read is no better off than the person who can't read. A Titan Life belongs to the learners. While food fuels your body, learning fuels your mind.

What should you read about? While reading novels about science-fiction, romance, mystery as a pastime is fine, if you want to live a Titan Life, I recommend you *read the biographies of the Titans you most admire and respect – and the books that shaped them!* This way, you will expose your mind to their Titan minds and their Titan ways of operating. Unlocking the power of these behaviors will put you one step closer to making the same things happen in your life.

While ordinary people love leisure and entertainment, Titans love education and applying the knowledge they learned. Thus, while ordinary people have gigantic TV sets at home, Titans have gigantic libraries at home. Invest in your personal library!

You cannot afford to buy books? First, instead of saying *"I can't afford it,"* which is a closed statement, ask yourself *"how could I afford it?"* And second, for you to start building your Titan Life now – not tomorrow – go to the public library!

If you "feel" that your life is already too overwhelming to find the time to read, wake up a little earlier or use your commute to listen to audiobooks.

How long should you read? Warren Buffett recommends reading 500 pages a day, but you will have to decide for yourself how much reading you do daily. Titans read at least 20 minutes a day! Here are some benefits of reading:

- **Expands your knowledge.** The more you know, the more you become.
- **Builds your wealth**. The more you learn, the more you can achieve.
- Increases **inspiration**.
- Expands **your vocabulary**.
- Makes **you a better writer.**
- Improves **your focus.**
- Helps you **revise your old paradigms and beliefs**.

- **Reduces stress.** No matter how much stress you have at work or in your personal relationships, it all slips away when you lose yourself in a good book.
- Provides you with **stronger analytical thinking skills.**
- **Stimulates the brain**, slowing or even preventing Alzheimer's and dementia.

T

TITAN BODY

Most of us, especially when we are younger, sacrifice health for wealth. And then, when we are sick, we would sacrifice every penny of our wealth for health.

Your energy is more valuable than your IQ. To build a Titan Life, you will need tons of energy! And you cannot have tons of energy if you are sick!

Titans think as professional athletes. They know that to perform at the top level, they must take care of their health.

While most people focus on "losing 20 pounds" or "not eating carbs" or "fasting," Titans focus on acquiring *life-enhancing habits.* Here are the areas Titans focus on:

- **Exercise.**
- **Eating.**
- **Sleep.**

Move!

We are becoming a society that gets sicker than ever before because we are not moving as much as we were designed to do.

For a longer and healthier life, it is not about the one who does the most exercise, but rather *the one who moves the most.*

If you look at the countries with the highest life expectancy – such as Japan, Spain and Italy – their citizens might not work out at the gym as much as the citizens of other countries, but they are constantly moving.

Whether you walk, ride a bicycle, dance, work in your vegetable garden, *moving every day is better than doing some strenuous exercise a few times a week,* and then sitting around, whether in your car, office or couch, for the rest of the day.

Your metabolism slows down 90% after thirty minutes of sitting. So stand more often throughout the day! And please, stop obsessing over getting in 10,000 steps a day! If the healthiest citizens of the world don't do this practice, why would you want to do it?

Work Out!

"It is exercise alone that supports the spirits,
and keeps the mind in vigor."

– Marcus Tullius Cicero

Besides moving every day, there are also Titan benefits to exercising at the gym 5 to 6 days a week!

The more fit you are, the more resilient your brain will function, and the more willpower you will develop. So get in Titan shape!

When you exercise, you create a cocktail of hormones (endorphins, serotonin, growth factors, dopamine) that are not only good for our physical health, but also for our mental one.

Contrary to popular belief, you do not need to work out for an hour each time. *Twenty to thirty minutes each day, when done consistently, are more effective than just two or three times a week for an hour each time.* The key is consistency!

Morning Exercise.

"An early-morning walk is a blessing for the whole day."
– Adam Smith

Titans know that to stay on top of their game, both personally and professionally, they must exercise regularly. Here's a list of Titans throughout history who have used exercise as a Titan tool: Hippocrates, Thomas Jefferson, Thomas Edison, John F. Kennedy, Warren Buffett, Richard Branson, Sylvester Stallone, Arnold Schwarzenegger, Bob Iger, Howard Schultz, Oprah Winfrey, Bill Gates, Mark Cuban, Tim Cook, Barack Obama, the list goes on.

Greek physician Hippocrates wrote, *"Even when all is known, the care of a man is not yet complete, because eating alone will not keep a man well; he must also take exercise. For food and exercise, while possessing opposite qualities, yet work together to produce health."*

John F. Kennedy stated, *"Physical fitness is not only one of the most important keys to a healthy body, it is the basis of dynamic and creative intellectual activity."*

And Barack Obama said, *"You have to exercise, or at some point you'll just break down."*

Why in the morning? Because after lying in bed for six, seven or eight hours, some morning exercise will help you *activate* your body!

Whether you like taking a walk, going for a run, lifting weights, doing yoga, swimming, gardening, *starting your day exercising is a great way to start your day*! Even if you work out later during the day, doing moderate exercise in the morning on an empty stomach for 20 minutes is a *game-changer* not only for your overall health (both physical and emotional) but also for your productivity! Here are some benefits of exercising in the morning:

- Improves **overall health.**
- Increases **metabolic rate.** You will burn fat much sooner!
- Brings **focus.**
- Helps build **discipline.**
- Improves **productivity.**
- Boosts **energy.**
- Improves **happiness and optimism.**
- Reduces **stress.**
- Improves **sleep.**
- Develops **brain.**
- Increases **motivation.**
- Promotes **courage.**
- Prolongs **life expectancy.**

A Titan Workout.

"The resistance that you fight physically in the gym and the resistance that you fight in life can only build a strong character."
– Arnold Schwarzenegger

Each workout should include a combination of cardio, mobility, strength, balance and stretching exercises.

For strengthening exercises, to get maximum results in minimum time, *antagonistic supersets are the best workout!*

This workout alternates exercises that target opposing muscle groups, like chest and back, quads and hamstrings, or biceps and triceps. This workout is not anything new. Arnold Schwarzenegger used antagonistic supersets in the 1970s, when training his way to winning seven Mr. Olympia trophies. Here are some of its benefits:

- **Muscular Balance.** While most people, especially guys, focus on their chest, shoulders and biceps, Titans focus on achieving muscular balance. The result, a more proportionate body and fewer injuries!
- **Increased Strength.** When you activate a muscle group, the antagonistic muscle group is inhibited to allow for greater force in the agonist. Through inhibition, you allow that muscle to restore its strength much quicker.
- **Time Efficient.** By pairing two opposing muscles like chest and back together, you can do more workout in a given time.

For better results, rest only between each pairing.

The Express Workout!

"Improvise, adapt and overcome!"
– Clint Eastwood

As we know, life is not always perfect and everything doesn't always go as planned. Had an emergency last night and slept in this morning? Traveling and not having a gym nearby? This is where the Express Workout comes in handy!

The Express Workout comprises 3 basic exercises:

- Push-ups.
- Sit-ups.
- Squats.

Do one superset of the trio, with ten, twenty, thirty, or a hundred reps of each exercise, depending on your physical condition.

Other Titan Tips For Exercising.

- **For better results, eliminate distractions** (TV, books, mobile phone. Only music is allowed.) For a workout to be effective, *you must focus all your energy on the muscle you are working.* In this sense, lifting weights is a great meditation!
- **Walk for at least twenty minutes** a day.
- **Use the stairs** instead of the elevator.
- **Change up your routine often.** Try attacking your muscles from different angles! In addition, it will prevent boredom. As they say, variety is the spice of life!
- **Breathe!** Many people seem to "stop breathing" when working out. Always exhale on exertion. For example, when pushing a bench press off your chest, you exhale on the push and inhale as you bring it slowly to your chest. When doing a pullup, you exhale on the pulling up motion and inhale on the way down.
- **Get a *2nd Titan Workout.*** This does not necessarily mean going to the gym again, but move when you leave work, whether you do some exercise, go for a walk, ride your bike, play with your children or do an *Express Workout.*
- **Reserve your treadmill for rainy days.** It is best to run outdoors! Yes, we must be careful about being in

the sun for long, but a bit of sun exposure, every day, is essential for your health and immune system.

- **Make recovery nutrition part of your training.** Don't go to practice or the gym without bringing a post-workout snack with you.
- **Get a massage once a week.** It will keep you healthy and more productive. Here are some of its benefits:
  - Improves your circulation.
  - Brings oxygen to your body's cells.
  - Helps the lymphatic system rid your body of toxicity.
  - Boosts your immune system.
  - Improves your sleep.

Eating.

"Let food be thy medicine and medicine be thy food."
– Hippocrates

The worldwide obesity rate has tripled since 1975. And yet, we spend billions of dollars annually on diet and weight loss products, and every year there's a new fashionable diet on the best seller list: *Atkins, Paleo, South Beach, Low-carb, Low-fat, Low-glycemic, Fasting,…*

Instead of listening to what the "experts" say about the latest diet, it would be wiser to look at the empirical evidence and see what the world's healthiest citizens eat. And the one thing that all of these regions have in common is they eat *real food!*

A simple rule of thumb is *food must come from either earth or a mother.* Anything else was probably invented in a laboratory in the last twenty years! No man-made food will ever replace natural food.

It's Not About Your Genes...

"Just like a single cell, the character of our lives is determined not by our genes but by our responses to the environmental signals that propel life."

– Bruce Lipton

For those of you who might think, *'Well, the world's healthiest citizens simply have better genes than me. That's all!'* I'm sorry to say, but according to the empirical evidence, this is not the case!

The citizens of Okinawa, Japan, enjoy one of the longest life expectancies in the world. If having a long and healthy life were about genes, Okinawans would live long lives no matter what they ate. But many Okinawans who migrated to the United States and adopted an "American-style" diet did not enjoy such long lives.

What you eat and drink over a long period of time affects your DNA, and yes, *it can activate or deactivate your body's longevity gene!*

"War On Carbs."

"Sooner or later a false belief bumps up against solid reality, usually on a battlefield."

– George Orwell

For the past fifteen years, carbohydrates have been labeled as public health enemy number one in the United States by many popular diet books, websites, and "health gurus." They have even been linked to even causing the country's obesity epidemic.

If we look at the citizens of the healthiest countries – Japan, Spain, Italy –, they eat noodles, rice and pasta! And, for the most part, they are quite lean as well!

You can actually lose body fat while on a high-carb diet. And, you can do so while also improving your energy and athletic performance simultaneously. Carbs are even good for your brain! *So carbs are not the enemy!* The enemy is the processed sauces that usually accompany the carbs. When making pasta, use natural tomato sauce, home-made pesto sauce or olive oil and a bit of grated parmesan cheese.

Fad Diets & Fasting.

"Healthy eating is a way of life, so it's important to establish routines that are simple, realistically, and ultimately livable."
– Horace

Whether *Atkins, Paleo, South Beach, Low-carb, Low-fat, Low-glycemic,... diets are not sustainable in the long-term.*

Many people try too hard following diets to lose weight and once they have reached their "ideal" weight, when they finish the diet, they return to the habits they had before, which makes them gain the weight they had before, and even multiply it. This is "rebound effect."

The same happens to *fasting.* While you might lose some weight right away, fasting is not sustainable in the long term. In addition, if you are fasting to lose weight, this is not the best practice in the long term as your body, uncertain of when the next meal will come, will go into "starvation protection" mode, slowing your metabolism and conserving calories, storing fat, and burning muscle (not fat) for energy.

Once again, if we look at the world's healthiest citizens, none of them fast. The citizens of Okinawa – the region with the highest number of supercentenarians – believe that *you should never starve yourself.*

If you are fasting for your religious belief, fine. But if you are fasting to lose weight or stay healthy, look somewhere else!

Some people swear by fasting – or intermittent fasting – for its "regenerative effect on the intestines." If you want to give your intestines a respite, go vegetarian (vegetables, fruits, cereals, beans, juice, tea) once a week. This helps cleanse the digestive system and allows it to rest. But do not starve yourself!

To have a long and healthy life, *we must not focus on following temporary fads, but on implementing long-term Titan habits.*

A Titan ~~Diet~~ Way of Eating.

"When diet is wrong, medicine is of no use. When diet is correct, medicine is of no need."
– *Ayurvedic Proverb*

Whatever you eat or drink should be intended to nourish your body.

As a general rule, the less packaging a food has, the better. A food with no package is your Titan choice! In addition, you must eat a bit of everything. *If you look at the world's healthiest countries such as Japan and Spain, their citizens eat variety.*

Okinawans – the region with the most supercentenarians – eat an average of 18 different foods each day! Spaniards – who enjoy the second-highest expectancy in the world and are expected to overtake Japan's long-held position by 2040 – have the concept of *tapas,* in which food is presented in small plates.

Let's look at the different Titan food groups:

Fruits and Vegetables.

This should be at the base of your food pyramid.

The world's healthiest citizens eat, on average, seven servings of fruits and vegetables daily.

Higher fruit and vegetable intake is linked to a lower risk of heart disease, cancer, diabetes, arthritis and some brain disorders. In addition, increased fruit intake is linked to lower blood-pressure, reduced oxidative stress and improved blood sugar control.

Eat the rainbow! Each color in fruits and vegetables is caused by specific phytonutrients, which are natural chemicals that help protect plants from germs, bugs, the sun's harmful rays, and other threats. Each color indicates an abundance of specific nutrients. So not only should you have a piece of fruit or vegetables with every meal or snack, but also you should try eating all kinds of vegetables and fruits!

For those concerned about the "sugar" in fruits, like the latest trendy diet claims, know this is *natural sugar*. This type of sugar has nothing to do with the added sugar in regular soda and many highly processed foods. When you eat fruits, their sugar comes wrapped in a fiber-rich, water-rich, nutrient-rich package. This fiber slows the release of fruit's natural sugar into your bloodstream, preventing a sugar spike, especially if you eat your fruit as part of a meal or snack.

So don't be afraid of eating fruits daily. They will not make you fat!

Eat More Fish Than Meat.

Fish is one of the staple foods in Japan and Spain, two of the world's healthiest countries.

The high levels of omega-3 fatty acids in oily fish have been associated with improved heart health.

What kind of fish should you eat? Here are some Titan choices: salmon, mackerel, sardines and albacore tuna. And, whenever possible, choose wild fish over farm-raised!

And if you will eat meat, poultry (chicken, turkey, duck) and wild game (buffalo, deer, elk) are better options than red meat (beef and pork). Reduce the consumption of red meat to once a week.

Legumes.

If you look at the world's healthiest countries, their citizens eat many legumes (soybeans, navy beans, chickpeas, lentils).

Legumes are a great source of fiber, vitamins, minerals and antioxidants. They have been associated with reducing the risk of heart disease, diabetes, cholesterol and even, certain cancers.

So eat legumes at least 2-3 times a week!

Nuts.

Nuts and seeds are high in antioxidants, minerals and healthy fats. They have been associated with a reduced risk of early death, heart disease and diabetes.

Here are some Titan choices: almonds, walnuts, sunflower seeds, pumpkin seeds and pistachios. And whenever possible, eat them raw, as opposed to roasted ᴜ fried.

So have some nuts, but don't go nuts over them! They are calorie-dense. A handful a day is plenty!

Whole Grains.

Whole grains contain many valuable nutrients, including fiber, B vitamins and minerals such as iron, magnesium and selenium.

Whole-grain consumption has also been associated with protection against cancer, heart disease, diabetes and obesity.

Here are some Titan options: oatmeal, barley, brown rice, buckwheat, millet, whole-wheat bread and whole-wheat pasta.

Fats.

Fats, especially of the monounsaturated kind, help lower your risk of heart disease, reduce inflammation, lower your cholesterol levels and are great for your hair and skin.

Here are some Titan choices: extra virgin olive oil (go for the cold-pressed version), avocados, nuts and eggs. John D. Rockefeller had a tablespoon of extra virgin olive oil daily, and he lived up to almost 98!

Just remember that monounsaturated fats are high in calories, so use them in moderation!

Ways Of Cooking.

        1 be cooked, except for sushi, nuts, fruits and
        ....s full of water. The preferable ways of
cooking are in this order:
1. Steamed.
2. Poached.
3. Boiled.
4. Baked.
5. Grilled.
6. Sautéed.

Limit your intake of barbecued or deep-fried foods. They are not only more difficult to digest, but also they have been linked to increasing the risk of developing cancer.

"Hara Bachi Bu."

Hara Bachi Bu is a Japanese term that could be roughly translated as "belly eighty percent full." It is a Confucian teaching that advises people to eat only until they are approximately eighty percent full.
    Never eat until you are "full." This will affect your energy levels. Be still a little hungry when you finish. It is not only better for your health, but it will also give you more energy and discipline.

Eat Less. Better Quality. More Frequently.

The key to a long and healthy life is to eat less, more frequently and with a higher nutritional content.

Overeating can change your metabolism – meaning how the cells in your body process the food you consume – and that can lead to chronic health problems, including diabetes. Smaller, more frequent meals are optimal.

Instead of eating two or three large meals a day, eat five or six smaller meals throughout the day. *Eating every three or four hours is the best way to be slim and healthy,* as this keeps your metabolism active and burning calories at a faster rate. In addition, having multiple smaller meals can help you make healthier choices, and avoid overeating, and will also stabilize your blood sugar levels throughout the day.

Another thing to remember is the quality of the food you are eating. Poor-quality food, meaning adulterated food, makes you fat and sick! The more natural and cleaner your "fuel" is, the smoother your "machine" will run.

How You Eat.

How you eat is as important as what you eat. If you look at the world's healthiest countries, the focus on the whole eating experience. Even if they sometimes eat fatty foods such as *rafute, jamón ibérico, ossobuco,* they sit at the table with friends and family, take one-hour meals, eat slowly and moderate portions, chew well, and perhaps, most importantly, eat with pleasure and appreciation.

Another thing to consider is that tension and stress from selecting the "perfect" food can cause restrictions in channels of the digestive organs, resulting in nutrient receiving malfunction. We are able to eat some "impure" food to strengthen our elimination organs. We are also designed to contract germs to build up our immune system.

So select the best foods you can, but if sometimes, healthy food is not available, then eat whatever you have with joy!

Drink.

The average adult human body is 50-65% water. Therefore, you need to stay well hydrated throughout the day. *Water is the ideal source of hydration.*

How much water do you need to drink a day? Rather than religiously documenting every ounce of fluid intake, let's keep things simple and do as the world's healthiest citizens do: *drink liquids with your meals and whenever you feel thirsty.* It doesn't mean you can "only" drink water to stay hydrated. Fresh fruit juices and milk are Titan options as well!

For drinking water, choose mineral water over its purified counterpart. For drinking juices, choose freshly squeezed over concentrate. If you like drinking milk, goat's milk is better than cow's milk, as the protein in goat's milk is closer to the protein in human milk, and thus, it is easier to digest.

Aside from water, fresh fruit juices and milk, here are other Titan options that the world's healthiest citizens drink: coffee, green tea and red wine. These are rich in antioxidants!

So do as the citizens of the healthiest countries do, and add some coffee, green tea and red wine to your life!

Alcohol.

Alcohol should be consumed in moderation and always accompanied by food.

When it comes to alcoholic drinks, red wine is your Titan option! Red wine is full of antioxidants that are good for your heart, brain, bone and immune system.

In Spain and Italy, two of the world's healthiest countries, the locals drink 1 or 2 glasses of red wine a day, but always accompanied by food!

So have a small glass of red wine, but make sure that it is some great wine. Life is too short for cheap wine! And if you can choose the organic version, so much better. All the good benefits that red wine has go away if it's full of toxics!

Have a Cheat Day.

Look, everyone's going to break down and have some ice cream sooner or later. We all have our inner child! The idea here is to plan to cheat. *Have a cheat day once a week – or one meal per week, up to you! – where you eat what you want.* One day of cheating a week is OK. As always, it's about what you do most of the time!

Other Titan Tips For Eating.

- **Eat organic** as much as you can. Organic is the new way of saying "the way mother nature intended it."
- **Avoid** eating at places where **"supersize" or "drive-thru"** are options.
- Order nothing off a menu that starts with **"fried"** or ends in **"fries."**
- **Eat less than 10 grams of salt per day**. Remember that many foods already have salt added. Mediterranean sea salt is your Titan option!

- **Stay away from salad dressings!** Here are some Titan options for dressings: cold-pressed extra virgin olive oil with balsamic, sherry or apple cider vinegar and sea salt, or cold-pressed extra virgin olive oil with lemon juice and sea salt.
- **Stay away from processed or frozen foods.** The occasional organic pizza for a lazy day where you don't feel like cooking is OK.
- **Rarely eat sugar.** *Honey is a much better option*! If you do eat sugar, choose cane sugar, as opposed to refined sugar or artificial sweeteners.
- **Whole wheat bread** is better than white bread.
- **Pork, in small portions,** is OK once or twice a week.
- **Dark chocolate** is better over milk chocolate. Dark chocolate's many antioxidants are good for your heart and brain health.
- **Never skip breakfast!**
- **Don't eat right before bed.** Your dinner should be around 3 hours before bedtime. If you couldn't have dinner, eat something light. Some Titan options are milk, cottage cheese, banana, kiwi, oatmeal, walnuts, almonds or fatty fish like a can of tuna or sardines.
- **Eat seasonable foods.** If you are not sure about what foods are seasonable, go to a farmers' market. Whatever they are selling, it is seasonal!
- **Make a grocery list.** What you didn't bring from the grocery store, you can't eat.
- **Eat at home as often as you can.** It's better for your health and for your finances!
- **Don't eat anything your great-grandmother wouldn't recognize as food**. This tip is from author Michael Pollan. If your great-grandmother would not recognize something as food, then it probably means

it was created in a lab a few years ago. Therefore, *it is not food!*

- Oh, one more thing! If you don't know, **smoking or vaping is bad for you!**

Sleep

"I treat sleep with as much respect as I treat food, or my training schedule, or my rivals. It's that important."
– Novak Djokovic

Everything starts with a good night's sleep! Titans are very aware of the importance of sleep. Roger Federer sleeps around twelve hours a day. LeBron James sleeps between eight and ten hours a day. Usain Bolt claims to sleep somewhere between nine and a half to ten hours a night, and he takes naps strategically during the day.

Sleep is not only for physical recovery but also for mental clarity and increased productivity and creativity. Einstein slept about ten hours a night. And Jeff Bezos makes sure to get eight hours of sleep every night.

Top models sleep between nine and ten hours, and the world's healthiest citizens sleep between 7 and 9 hours of sleep a day.

So whether it is for physical or mental performance, beauty or health, sleep is extremely important! *It restores your energy and heals your body and mind.*

Pursuing a Titan Life, however you define it, is rarely a sprint. You must be in it for the long haul, like a marathon. And sleep plays a key role in that marathon!

The 8-Hour Myth.

*"Each night, when I go to sleep, I die. And the next
morning, when I wake up, I am reborn."*

— *Mahatma Gandhi*

According to Nick Littlehales, elite sport sleep coach to Cristiano Ronaldo, Real Madrid, Manchester United and Arsenal Football Club, *we, humans, sleep in 90-minute cycles.*

Under clinical-trial conditions, this has shown to be the amount of time required to complete one full cycle through the stages of sleep. But, *how you clock in the number of daily cycles you need to function best is up to you and your schedule.*

Littlehales uses that figure to guide the entire evening, with each 90-minute block equal to one cycle. So, two cycles is three hours of sleep, three cycles equals four and a half hours of sleep, and so on.

Considering that we sleep in 90-minute cycles, *aim for either six, seven and a half, or nine hours of sleep each night.*

What's the right amount of sleep for you? As with anything else, there is not a one-size-fits-all answer to this question. It depends on each individual case. If after sleeping for six hours, you still feel moody, tired, get sick easily, then try adding another 90-minute cycle to your sleep!

Littlehales recommends getting, *at least, thirty-five cycles – or five cycles per night – in a given week.* For example, if on a particular night you only get four or even three cycles - six hours of sleep or less, you can add on a full 90-minute cycle or two later on in the week when your schedule is less demanding.

Titan Bedtime And Wake Up Time.

*"Early to bed and early to rise, makes a man
healthy, wealthy, and wise."*
— *Benjamin Franklin*

While everyone is different, the evidence suggests that *the ideal sleep schedule should mimic the sun's rising and falling, depending on where you are on the planet.*

One of the best ways to figure out your Titan bedtime is to do the math backward in ninety-minute cycles. In addition, consider adding around fifteen minutes for your body to fall asleep. For instance, let's say you want to wake up at 6:00 AM. Your Titan bedtime would be either 11:45 PM (for a 6-hour sleep), 10:15 PM (for a 7.5-hour sleep) or 8:45 PM (for a 9-hour sleep).

Whatever bedtime you decide, as a general rule, *make sure you are sleeping before midnight.* For reasons that go beyond the scope of this book, going to sleep before midnight is good for your overall health.

Some experts suggest that the deepest and most regenerative sleep occurs between 10:00 PM and 2:00 AM. Therefore, you should be sleeping by 10:00 PM, as this is the time your body goes through a transformation following the rise in melatonin production.

So if you want to shoot for getting seven and a half hours of sleep, it is better to sleep those seven and a half hours from 10:00 PM to 5:30 AM than from 12:00 PM to 7:30 AM. As with anything else, it is about the quality, not the quantity!

The Power Of Power Naps.

"Always nap when you can. It is cheap medicine."
— *Lord Byron*

What did Margaret Thatcher, Thomas Edison, Salvador Dali, John F. Kennedy, Eleanor Roosevelt, Winston Churchill, Leonardo da Vinci and Albert Einstein have in common? They were all nappers! Some of history's greatest minds have used naps to help them get their jobs done.

Studies show that mid-day naps can improve your mood and boost productivity. In many of the world's healthiest countries a midday nap is common.

About 6 hours after you wake up, your circadian rhythm dips, and an afternoon nap is a life changer! The ideal time for midday napping is after lunch, no later than 2:00 PM; its ideal duration is between 20-30 minutes. Unless you need to add a full 90-minute cycle to catch up with your sleep.

Companies such as Facebook, Google and NASA have nap rooms at their headquarters. If you can't nap at work, use 5-10 min of your lunch break to close your eyes and relax. This will help you conquer the after-lunch sleepy state.

To reap the mind-focusing benefits naps can offer, you don't even need to fall asleep to; simply resting or meditating for a few minutes provides the same results.

Other Titan Tips For Sleeping.

- **Do not exercise before going to bed.** It will stimulate your nervous system and interfere with your sleep quality.
- **Your last meal and glass of wine** should be about three hours before going to bed.
- **Take a hot shower** or, better yet, a hot bath with Epsom salts an hour before your bedtime.

- **Turn off your electronic devices** – or put them airplane mode – at least ninety minutes befoɪ bedtime.
- **Try to keep a steady bedtime and wake-up time**, even on the weekends.
- **Keep a cool room** (around 65-70 °F or 18-21°C .)
- **Invest** in a great mattress, pillows and sheets.
- **No work in the bedroom.** Only sleep, reading, Titan conversations with your partner and sex are allowed!
- **Avoid caffeine** at least eight hours before bedtime.
- **Drink relaxation tea** after dinner.
- **Dim the lights** in your house around three hours before bedtime.
- **Shut out the lights** in your room. The darker the room, the better.
- **Celebrate your victories** of the day!

T

TITAN HEART

"Develop the heart. Too much energy in your country is spent developing the mind, instead of the heart. Be compassionate. Not just to your friends, but to everyone."

— Dalai Lama

A Titan Life is about loving and being loved. If you do nothing else, *having connections with people is a game-changer to your happiness.* Look at children. They are not thinking about improving their mind, their body, their finances and yet, they are their happiest when they play and interact with other children.

J. Paul Getty was, at one time, considered the world's richest man. During the most active years in his business, he lived alone in a 72-room mansion outside London. According to one of his wives, he spent so much time building a business he had no time to build a relationship with his family. At the end of his life, this is how J. Paul Getty felt, *"I hate to be a failure. I would gladly give all my millions for just one, lasting marital success."*

You could have a great mind — and all the money in the world, but if you have no one to share it with, it will be an empty victory, and you will never be truly happy.

We, as a society, have become so self-centered that we neglect everyone around us, including our spouse, our children, our parents, our friends and our community in pursuit of our selfish goals. We have got to the point where if two fellow human beings pass by each other on a lonely sidewalk, they won't say hello to each other or even make eye contact!

Most people are working for selfish ends, not caring about others, and this alone has brought much misery in the world today. Can we really be surprised that rates of anxiety, depression and unhappiness are so high? This is a human crisis!

So how can we develop a Titan Heart? *By forming Titan human connections.* And how do we form Titan connections? *By putting their interests above your own.*

- Do you want to have a Titan marriage? Put your spouse's interest above your own.
- Do you want to have a Titan family? Put your family's interests above your own.
- Do you want to have Titan friendships? Put your friends' interests above your own.
- Do you want to have a Titan community? Put your community's interests above your own.

To develop a Titan Heart, we must stop thinking about ourselves and start thinking about others. In the words of Bruce Lee, *"Real living is living for others."*

A Titan Marriage.

"The whole is greater than the sum of its parts."
– Aristotle

For this book, "marriage" is defined as the union of two souls to form a new Titan one. Under this definition, no formal ceremony or rite is needed.

When the "right" two people come together to work towards a common goal – a Titan Life together – the results will be astonishing! Hence, a Titan Marriage can make 1+1 = 3!

We all know that cooperative effort produces power, but *cooperative effort based upon total harmony of purpose develops Titan power*! Here are some Titan marriages throughout history:

Four married couples have jointly received the Nobel Prize for their scientific research: Pierre and Marie Curie, Gunnar and Alva Myrdal, Carl and Gerti Cori, and Frederic and Irene Joliot.

Frances Goodrich and Albert Hackett were a *Pulitzer Prize* and *Academy Award-winning* husband and wife.

Of course, there are also situations where a husband and wife don't do the exact same thing, but where the maxim of *"Behind every great man is a great woman"* holds true:

Sophia Tolstaya (Leo Tolstoy), Clementine Ogilvy Spencer (Winston Churchill), Mercedes Barcha Pardo (Gabriel García Márquez) and Elena Diakonov "Gala" (Salvador Dalí), among others. In these instances, these women were modest, self-denying wives, of whom the public heard but little or nothing, but who supported their husbands to become the Titans they became!

The Most Important Ingredient In A Marriage.

"Only humility knows how to appreciate and admire the good qualities of others."
– Sri Chinmoy

The most important ingredient in a marriage is *humility*. From the time you are born, you build up ego to survive and defend yourself when the occasion calls for it. But then, when you marry someone, you have to leave the ego at the door before you walk inside your house. Thus, marrying someone – and making the marriage work – is the most selfless act you can do.

Every fight between married couples, from the time of Adam and Eve down to today, stems from pride and self-centeredness. What many couples fail to understand is that *a Titan marriage is about developing a mutual admiration, a deep respect and an awareness of the other person's needs.*

Time and experience have proven that humility is the key to a Titan marriage for it invites reasoning together. Marriage is the cure to pride and selfishness because it forces a person to get out of themselves and tend to their spouse. So if you want to have a Titan marriage, *be humble and put your spouse's interest above your own.*

"Kaizen" Also Applies To Marriages.

"Coming together is a beginning; keeping together is progress; working together is success." – Henry Ford

A Titan Marriage is about *mutual improvement.* It's about helping each other grow, expand and improve. It's about helping each other become better and reach your personal Titan goals. By doing this, you are not only benefitting each individual spouse, but also you are strengthening the marriage as a whole.

For this, *you must be able to only give criticism to uplift or build the marriage.* Yes, you have the right – and duty – to call your spouse out when you see they are out of line. But this must be done with consideration for the thoughts and feelings of the other person. Love is so fragile, it must be handled with much care!

A Titan Marriage is achieved when spouses not only grow but grow together, achieving a Titan oneness.

Finding A Titan Companion.

"Being deeply loved by someone gives you strength, while loving someone deeply gives you courage."

– *Lao Tzu*

Whether you choose to formally get married or not – this is up to you - *traveling in pairs through life is one of the best ways of finding happiness.* Back in the day, traveling involved a lot of risks, and traveling companions were for security, not just for fun. A marriage is the same. In the journey through life, a sorrow shared is half a sorrow; a joy shared is twice a joy. Now the key is to make sure you find the right traveler companion! Here are some simple rules for finding your Titan companion:

1. Become a Titan if you want to attract a Titan.

Often, we make mental – sometimes real – checklists of the attributes that our ideal spouse should have: "He should be considerate, attractive, smart, well-educated, funny, rich." But seldom do we cultivate these attributes ourselves!

Considering that you attract to yourself people similar to you, the surest way to attract a spouse with a certain set of attributes is to *start by developing said attributes yourself!*

When I hear people saying, *"I'm so unlucky! I always attract the wrong person!"* Well, guess who the wrong person is? To attract Mr. Titan, you first have to become Mrs. Titan, and vice versa!

2. Find someone you enjoy talking to.

This piece of advice comes from an older Japanese business Titan I met years ago. He said, *"When looking for a wife, look for someone who you enjoy talking to. Because, in the end, this is what you two will do most of the time."*

3. Will she (he) change your diaper?

And the final piece of advice, though a bit scatological, comes from a Spanish business Titan who, years ago, said to me, *"When looking for the right spouse, ask yourself, 'if I were to become disabled, would she (he) change my diaper?'"*

I will let you ponder over these three.

Other Tips For Developing A Titan Marriage.

- **Have daily meetings with your spouse** to discuss your professional projects, finances and home life.
- **Have quarterly and yearly retreats** with your spouse to take a break and to discuss your future plans, family trips, family projects.
- **Schedule a weekly date** with your spouse.
- **Add adventure into your marriage:** try new experiences together, stop the car and pick some wildflowers, book a hotel in your own city, serve her a surprise breakfast in bed, have an improvised picnic, send her a love note, dress sexy for him.
- **Do things together your spouse enjoy**, even if you don't enjoy them! Don't concentrate on the activity itself; focus on the bond that grows out of sharing the experience with your spouse.
- **Speak highly of your spouse** in front of others, especially your children.

- **Let go of having to be always right.** As Cato the Elder said, *"I think the first virtue is to restrain the tongue; he approaches nearest to gods who knows how to be silent, even though he is in the right."*

Titan Sex

"Good sex is like good bridge. If you don't have a good partner, you'd better have a good hand."

– Mae West

Most people focus on their own pleasure and time frame, rather than a mutual experience. This is the wrong approach!

Titan Sex happens when a person is whole-heartedly seeking to fulfill his partner's needs and desires and, vice-versa. *When both are seeking to sexually please the other, then Titan Sex is born!*

When both partners are being selfless, you have a deeper connection and sexual intimacy. If you focus on the other person having a satisfying sexual experience, they will want to give you a satisfying experience right back. When you put your partner's interest above your own, it shows them you are thinking about their desires and needs. And when your partner sees this, more than likely, they will mirror that attitude towards you.

So if you want to have Titan sex, *put your partner's interest above your own.*

Channeling Your Sex Energy.

"People ask me a lot about my drive. I think it comes from, like, having a sexual addiction at a really young age. Look at the drive that people have to get sex – to dress like this and get a haircut and be in the club in the freezing cold at 3 a.m., the places they go to pick up a girl. If you can focus the energy into something valuable, put that into work ethic."

– Kanye West

Titans are usually men and women with highly developed sex natures, who have learned to channel their sex energy to build Titan things. *Sex energy is the creative energy of all Titans.*

According to Napoleon Hill, *"the main reason the majority of men who succeed do not do so before the age of 40-50 is their tendency to dissipate their energies through over-indulgence in the physical expression of the emotion of sex."*

The desire for sexual expression cannot and should not be submerged or eliminated, but it should be *channeled* from a desire for physical contact into some other form of desire and action.

Channeling your sex energy calls for much willpower than the average person is willing to use, but the reward is worth the effort for building your Titan Life!

When the emotion of love and romance are mixed with the emotion of sex, a person is lifted to the status of a Titan!

A Titan Family.

"Without a family, man, alone in the world, trembles with the cold."
– Andre Maurois

Family is the basis. Nothing is more important than family. Many Titans throughout history have been aware of the importance of having a family: Friedrich Nietzsche, George Bernard Shaw, Albert Schweitzer, Albert Einstein, Walt Disney, Albert Camus, Jane Howard, Maya Angelou, Warren Buffett, Richard Branson, Bill Gates and Jeff Bezos, among many others.

Jane Howard said, *"Call it a clan, call it a network, call it a tribe, call it a family: Whatever you call it, whoever you are, you need one."*

Walt Disney stated, *"A man should never neglect his family for business."*

Albert Einstein said, *"Rejoice with your family in the beautiful land of life."*

And Bill Gates, when asked about his definition of success, quoted his friend by saying: *"Warren Buffett has always said the measure is whether the people close to you are happy and love you."*

If all you connect is with people at the office, even if you get along well, your life will be unidimensional, not Titan!

When asked, most people say that their family is important to them. But the question is, *why aren't they in your schedule?*

Spend time with your loved ones. Show them your love! Do activities together! It's not about the quantity but the quality of the time you spend. Don't be just a "family man." *Be the creator of Titan moments with your family!*

Be Present With Your Loved Ones.

"The most precious gift we can offer others is our presence. When mindfulness embraces those we love, they will bloom like flowers."
– Thich Nhat Hanh

Being present is the greatest gift you can give to your loved ones. *To be present is to engage physically, mentally, emotionally and spiritually in a given moment.*

Instead of thinking about things you need to do, or things that have happened to you, or worrying or planning or regretting, be present.

And please, don't forget to turn off your electronic devices if you want to be fully present with your loved ones!

Make Time For Titan Conversations.

"The real art of conversation is not only to say the right thing at the right place but to leave unsaid the wrong thing at the tempting moment."

– Dorothy Nevill

In a world that talks in texts, emails, over the phone and on social media, human conversations, face to face, are more needed than ever!

Conversations face to face release chemicals good for your brain. Nothing is like looking into each other's eyes as you talk to each other, witnessing each other's reactions and sharing emotions.

And remember to listen more than you speak. This is why you were given two ears and one mouth. So you can listen twice as much as you speak.

Other Tips For Developing A Titan Family.

- **Have breakfast with your loved ones.** There's no better way to start your day! If you can't afford this luxury, think of ways for you to afford it. Meanwhile, you can have dinner together.
- If you are away from home, **call your loved ones daily**. Even if it's only for 5 minutes, this is a game-changer to your happiness!
- **Schedule family trips** at the end of December for the entire year, and arrange your life around those family vacations.

- **Schedule daily family time.**
- **Schedule weekend activities** with your family.

Titan Children.

"Give the ones you love wings to fly,
roots to come back, and reasons to stay."
– Dalai Lama

Titan children are not the ones who are taught about love, but the ones who *experience love*. The result, they will grow into healthy, happy and well-adjusted adults.

Children grow incredibly quickly! Use that little window of time to enjoy them and develop them. Our job as parents is to inspire our children to build their own Titan Lives. So they can elevate the world and make it a better place!

To develop Titan Children, *put your children's interests above your own*. It's that simple. Not easy, but simple.

No one ever becomes an "expert" parent, but here are some Titan tips that you might find useful:

- **Believe in your children.** Children are likely to live up to what you believe of them.
- **Be the creator of Titan moments** with your family.
- **Take more pictures with the lens of your soul** than with the lens of your camera.
- **Keep your family close by**.
- **Give your children your undivided attention** when you are with them. This will boost their self-esteem.
- **Treat all your children** the same by treating them differently.
- **Keep your promises!** This will build bridges of trust.

- **Expose** your kids to Titan conversations, Titan books, Titan environments.
- **Teach them by example.** Children will not listen to what you say, but *they will watch what you do.*
- **Play with them,** or watch them play!
- **Have breakfast and dinner** with them.
- **Smile!** Even when you begin to lose your patience with them, the very act of smiling will not let you steam and lose your temper.
- **Participate** in the things they enjoy doing, even if it is to watch their favorite shows or movies.
- **Spend quality time** with your child. No need for big slots of time!
- **Be a hero to your kids.** Remember, heroes are not necessarily the best in business.
- **Listen to your kids.**
- **Encourage** your kids to do what they love.
- **Schedule private dates** with each one of your children.
- **Keep a secret Victory Logbook** of your child's accomplishments to be handed to them at an important occasion in their life, such as graduation, marriage…

Titan Friendships.

"Friendship: The glory of friendship is not the outstretched hand, nor the kindly smile, nor the joy of companionship; it's the spiritual inspiration that comes to one when he discovers that someone else believes in him and is willing to trust him with his friendship."
– Ralph Waldo Emerson

One thing that most people seem to fail to understand is that friendships – like any other relationship – are like plants. You must nurture them for them to grow. *Developing Titan friendships take time and effort.*

Friends are the family we choose. Like William Shakespeare said, *"A friend is one that knows you as you are, understands where you have been, accepts what you have become, and still, gently allows you to grow."*

Nothing is like a good conversation with a good friend, but even better, nothing is like a good silence with a good friend.

If you have a Titan friend, you are an extremely lucky person! A Titan friend shows his love in times of trouble, not only in times of happiness. Like Oprah Winfrey said, *"Lots of people want to ride with you in the limo, but what you want is someone who will take the bus with you when the limo breaks down."*

On your journey to the mountaintop, don't forget to take your Titan friends with you!

Other Tips For Developing Titan Friendships.

- **Be the best friend** you can be.
- **Be dependable**. Be loyal to those not in your presence and you will create a higher level of trust with those who are in your presence.
- **Don't criticize or gossip**. Average people talk about others. Titans talk about dreams and ideas.
- Don't be on time, **be early!**
- **Be just.** In a society plagued with apathy, those who stand up for themselves or others will stand out.
- **Reconnect** with old friends.

- **Nurture your friendships** often: drink a glass of wine or a cup of tea or coffee, sing together, talk about life.
- **Have fun together, at least once, a month**: share a hobby, a workout together, go to dance.
- **Go "the extra mile,"** even if it involves traveling when a friend is in times of trouble.
- **Develop a Titan circle of friends.** Commit to meeting Titans like you!

A Titan Reputation.

"It takes 20 years to build a reputation and five minutes to ruin it. If you think about that, you'll do things differently."
– Warren Buffett

Most people do what's easy. Titans do what's right! Titans know there is nothing more important than a good name and going to sleep with a clear conscience.

You will never go wrong if you do what's right. It might take you longer to accomplish your goals, but don't lose your reputation on your way to the top. Nothing is more important than knowing you have travelled with a sense of integrity.

One great tool to build a Titan reputation is the *newspaper test.* Simply put, act as if everything you do were to be written in the newspapers and read by your family, friends and neighbors. Would you still do it? Whenever you doubt whether to do a particular action, do the newspaper test.

How Titan are you when no one is watching? Have the strength of character to do the right thing, even when no one is watching you. *You can afford to lose money, but you can't afford to lose your reputation.*

A Titan Community.

*"Man is by nature a social animal; an individual who is
unsocial naturally and not accidentally is either beneath our
notice or more than human. Society is something that precedes
the individual. Anyone who either cannot lead the common life
or is so self-sufficient as not to need to, and therefore does not
partake of society, is either a beast or a god. "*

– Aristotle

Human connections are fundamental for living a Titan Life.
If you do nothing else, having connections with other human
beings, even if they are "strangers," is a game-changer to
your happiness – and theirs! As Pablo Casals said, *"To the
world you may be one person; but to one person you may be
the world.*

Just as it is reassuring to have a companion when
traveling, it is important for us to care for each other as we
pass through life.

If we look at the healthiest countries, they have a strong
sense of community. This is what the citizens of Ogimi,
Okinawa – the place with the highest number of
supercentenarians – call *icharibachode*, which means, "treat
everyone like a brother, even if you've never met them
before." My wife and I had the privilege of visiting Ogimi,
Okinawa, and they sure made us feel like a sister and brother,
even though they had just met us!

This sense of community, belonging and support gives the
individual a sense of security that seems to increase not only
their happiness but also their life expectancy.

We humans all have something in common, and that is
our *humanness*. And the day we are to recognize that, we
will have a Titan world!

Rethinking "Stranger Danger."

"A friend may be waiting behind a stranger's face."

– Maya Angelou

For those who are not familiar with "stranger danger," this is the idea or warning that all strangers can be potentially dangerous. Children in some parts of the world learn this at a young age. While well-intentioned, this is devastating to the child's development! One thing is to teach our kids some basic street smarts, and a completely different one is to teach them to fear everyone they don't know. No wonder, when these children later become adults, it is not unusual for them to pass by each other on a lonely sidewalk, and not say hello to each other or even make eye contact!

To those adults who were part of the "stranger danger" generation, I have a little secret for you: *Talking to "strangers" makes you happy!* The best way to avoid anxiety and depression, and to be happy is to go out in the street and say hello to people with a big smile on your face. People who talk to strangers – in coffee shops, in lines at the post office, while walking down the street and passing by another fellow human being – feel more connected to those around them.

And if you have children, teach them to say hello to strangers. It not only helps them develop good social skills, but they will grow into happier adults! As the African proverb says, *"It takes a village to raise a child."*

Other Tips For Developing A Titan Community.

- **Respect and promote all religions**, even if you are not religious. Surround yourself by an eclectic religious atmosphere and search for insights from different religious traditions.
- **Take down your social mask** and let your humanity come out. People around you will most likely do the same.
- **Make eye contact** when you talk to someone.
- **Say *Hello* and *Good-bye*.** It means 'I acknowledge you.'
- **Say *Please*.** It means 'I respect you.'
- **Say *Thank you*.** It means 'I appreciate you.'
- **Listen more than you speak.** As Jorge Luis Borges said, *"Do not speak unless you can improve the silence."*
- **Compliment strangers.**
- **Talk to old people.** There is no one wiser, more experienced, than those who have lived through life.
- **Self-respect** is the best means of getting the respect of others. Don't ask for respect. Earn it!
- **Be of service** to your community.

Titan Emotions.

*"Some people come into your life as a
blessing, others come into your life as a lesson."*
– *Mother Teresa*

You cannot build a Titan Life if you are full of emotional toxicity. Any suppressed or repressed emotions you don't deal with will eventually show its ugly face in not only

unhappiness but also illnesses. This is v
importance *you deal with these emotic*
possible!

As obvious as this may sound, this is
by most people. They think that only by
minds, they can live a Titan Life. Nothing could be further
from the truth! *Repression and suppression are destroying
your Titan Life.*

Every emotion is intelligent. This is why you must listen
to them! To work on your emotional baggage, *journaling is
a Titan tool.* Write about your emotions. Get to know them.
When something hurts, ask yourself, *'Where does this come
from?'* Deconstruct it. Cry if you feel like it. And take
action! Only then will you be able to live a Titan Life!

Open your heart to the world. I know you have been
emotionally hurt, abused in some way in the past, but know
that *the vines stressed the most, make the greatest wines.*

Conflict is just growth waiting to happen. *Titans use their
traumas as fertilizer to grow and become Titan.* What is the
most natural fertilizer after all? As nature transforms animal
feces into nourishing energy, you can do the same with your
traumas!

The only people with no problems are dead. The painful
experiences make you grow. Like Kahlil Gibran said, *"The
deeper the sorrow carves into your being, the more joy you
can contain."*

So forgive and ask for forgiveness, fall in love and let
others fall in love with you. Open your heart, not only to your
family and friends, but to humanity. This is how you build a
Titan Life!

Other Tips For Developing A Titan Heart.

- **When in a heated argument**, don't say anything. You might regret it later on! Take a walk outside. Let the engines cool down. Hurting words are difficult to forget. They might be forgiven, but they are difficult to forget.
- **Develop understanding, empathy and compassion** for others and, also, for yourself!
- With love, **be willing to take risks, yes, again!**
- **Never be defined by your past.** It was just a lesson, not a life sentence. As Beyoncé said, *"Embrace mistakes. They make you who you are."*

T

TITAN SKILL

"By blood, I'm Albanian. By citizenship, an Indian. By faith,
I am a Catholic nun. As to my calling, I belong to the world."
— Mother Teresa

A Titan Skill is your "reason for being." This is what the Japanese call your *ikigai*; the French call it your *raison d'être*; others call it "your calling;" and author Paulo Coelho calls it "your personal legend." Whatever you call it, you need to find one! Why? Because *although your skill isn't your life, it will fill a large part of it.*

Your Titan Skill is your shot at immortality, besides being a great source of confidence, self-worth, recognition, happiness, and yes, money!

Most people reverse the order. They want to be rich, famous, awarded, confident. What they fail to realize is that *money, recognition, awards, and self-confidence are byproducts of your level of mastery at your craft.*

If you are struggling financially, it only means you are mediocre at what you do for a living. If you are making a decent living, it means that your level of expertise is, well, decent. Only those whose level of mastery equals that of a Titan will receive a Titan paycheck! *So don't focus on money or fame; focus on developing a Titan skill!*

Do What You Love.

"The only way to do great work is to love what you do. If you haven't found it yet, keep looking. Don't settle. As with all matters of the heart, you'll know when you find it. [...] Have the courage to follow your heart and intuition. They somehow already know what you truly want to become."

– Steve Jobs

Not sure what your Titan Skill may be? Ask yourself, '*What excites me? What brings me enthusiasm?*'

Most people pursue a career because of the financial opportunities or because their family consciously or unconsciously pushed them to follow the same path as they did. For example, working in the corporate world, children of doctors who become doctors. These people, especially if they stay long enough, might achieve some financial success, but they will never become the Titans of their fields, and most importantly, they will never be truly happy!

To become a Titan, you must make Titan sacrifices. And unless you are truly passionate about what you do, you will never achieve Titan status. Because what happens to most people is that, when things get difficult – as they will – they quit. Because they are "reasonable" human beings! *And who, in their right mind, would want to go through all that pain and suffering for so long, unless you love what you are doing?*

So find what you love! If you haven't found what you love yet, I encourage you to keep looking. Do the necessary inner work. Journal about it. *You have something unique that you can contribute to this world!* A good clue to find what you love is to go back in time and think about the things you were passionate about when you were a child. What were you obsessed about?

And once you find your Titan Skill, you will never have to "work" another day again, and you will never want to retire! Look at Warren Buffett, Richard Branson, Amancio Ortega, Larry Ellison, and Bill Gates. They are still at it because they love what they do! Loving what you do is the only way to become a Titan in your field. Like Aristotle said, *"Pleasure in the job puts perfection in the work."*

And when you find what you love, you will need less self-discipline and willpower. No one will have to push you to stay practicing on the weekends because your Titan Skill will pull you. Whatever you need to do to become a Titan in your field, you will happily do it! *Only then will you be able to defy the odds and achieve what others think is "impossible"*...

The Myth Of A Titan.

"I start early and I stay late, day after day, year after year. It took me 17 years and 114 days to become an overnight success."

– Leo Messi

Most people have romantic notions about athletes, writers and artists who became famous "overnight," seemingly because of their "natural talent." They look at Leo Messi, Rafael Nadal, Bill Gates, Elon Musk, and Kanye West, and they believe these people are "cut from a different cloth" and they are "naturally gifted." However, what most people fail to realize is that these Titans trained and practiced day-in and day-out for many years before they became an "overnight success."

Sam Snead, who was called "the best natural player ever," told *Golf Digest*, *"People always said I had a natural swing.*

They thought I wasn't a hard worker. But when I was young, I'd play and practice all day, then practice more at night by my car's headlights. My hands bled. Nobody worked harder at golf than I did."

Hard-work will always beat talent. Yes, you might have certain talents that come more naturally to you, but to become a Titan, you have to practice, practice and practice. There are no shortcuts!

Becoming a Titan is not about genes. It is about monomaniacal focus and obsessive practice on your Titan skill.

Act Like A Titan To Be One.

"Men acquire a particular quality by constantly acting in a particular way."

– Aristotle

As we now say, *fake it until you make it!* In the same way that we become more enthusiastic by acting more enthusiastic, you must act like a Titan to become one.

William James wrote, *"Act as if you are."*

Paulo Coelho stated, *"You must be the person you have never had the courage to be. Gradually, you will discover that you are that person, but until you can see this clearly, you must pretend and invent."*

And Lady Gaga said, *"I want people to walk around delusional about how great they can be. And then fight so hard for it every day that the lie becomes the truth."*

You don't need to trick anyone. *The only person you must trick is yourself.*

Instead of focusing on writing a book, focus on being a writer. *Because once you have adopted that identity, your actions will match your identity.* You will be acting in alignment with the type of person you already see yourself to be. You're not really motivating yourself that much. You're like, "This is who I am. This is why I do what I do." Any Titan achievement is about developing the identity and "being" that person before you become that person!

A Titan Obsession.

"There's no talent here, this is hard work. This is an obsession. Talent does not exist, we are all human beings. You could be anyone if you put in the time. You will reach the top, and that's that. I am not talented, I am obsessed."
– Conor Mc Gregor

Mediocre people call it a "job." Average people call it a "career." Excellent people call it a "mission." Titans call it an "obsession".

Until your craft is not an obsession, you will not become a Titan. You must be obsessed about your craft. You must read everything about your craft. Study the Titans in your field that came before you. You need to know more about your craft than anyone who has ever done the work you do in the history of the world. Practice day in and day out. Think, dream and eat your craft!

This is how Titans are made. There is no natural talent. There are no shortcuts. Be obsessed and put in the work, and the results will come!

Titan Work-Ethic.

"Only one who devotes himself to a cause with his whole strength and soul can be a true master. For this reason, mastery demands all of a person."
– Albert Einstein

Mastery is a process, not a destination. The only way you will become a Titan is if you develop a Titan work-ethic. As Picasso said, *"Inspiration exists, but it must find you working."*

Titans practice every day, whether they feel "motivated" and "inspired" or not. They show up every day, no matter what is going on – for good or ill – around them or inside them. They play hurt; they outwork everyone; they always deliver more than expected; and they have the three *Self's*: they are self-educated, self-motivated and self-made.

We all can become Titans, but most of us are not willing to make the sacrifices that will make us Titan. As they say, *everyone wants to go to heaven, but no one is willing to die.* And to become a Titan, you must be willing to die!

Titans Love Solitude.

"Without great solitude, no serious work is possible."
– Pablo Picasso

All Titans spend time in solitude for extended periods of time to develop their Titan Skill: Picasso, Edison, Einstein, Haruki Murakami, Daniel Day-Lewis, Kanye West all know that *a Titan Skill is made known silently when no one is looking. When the lights are out, and there is no applause.* This is how they produce Titan level of work.

Picasso disposed of the "obligations of friendship" in a single afternoon by inviting them for dinner all together, so he could devote more time to his craft!

To become a Titan, you'd better get used to being alone and working on your craft when no one is looking!

Schedule blocks of total solitude for you to do Titan level of work!

Run Your Own Race.

"Don't be the best in the world at what you do; be the only one in the world who does what you do."
— *Jerry Garcia*

Initially, study the Titans of your craft. Learn their techniques. Once you do, throw everything out of the window and find your own, original Titan style.

Every Titan differentiated themselves from the herd and marched to their own drumbeat. You will not connect with your muse by following the herd. Don't do what others do. Don't do what's expected. When you focus on your competition, you stop creating. Ask yourself, *"How can I create more value to my fans, readers, customers?"* Differentiate yourself from the crowd and competition. Change the status quo! One secret to becoming a Titan is to *do things in life never done before in the history of the world.*

You already have that unique quality in you. There is no one like you! Take advantage of your own uniqueness and gifts!

Carry A Notepad.

"If you don't write your ideas down, they could leave your head before you even leave the room."
— *Richard Branson*

Having a small notepad with you at all times could elevate you to the realm of Titans! Yes, you heard me well. By keeping an old-fashioned pen and a small notebook always handy, you can keep track of and remember all the ideas that come to you throughout the day.

As soon as an idea pops into your mind, write it down. Otherwise, it will vanish as quickly as it came to you!

Here's a list of Titans who were/are avid note-takers: Leonardo da Vinci, Benjamin Franklin, Thomas Jefferson, Ludwig van Beethoven, Charles Darwin, Mark Twain, John D. Rockefeller, Thomas Edison, Pablo Picasso, George Patton, Ernest Hemingway, Warren Buffet, George Lucas, Richard Branson, Bill Gates and J.K. Rowling, among others.

Richard Branson said, *"It may sound ridiculous, but my most important [tool] is to always carry a little notebook in your back pocket. [...] I can't tell you where I'd be if I hadn't had a pen on hand to write down my ideas as soon as they came to me."*

And Aristotle Onassis said, *"Always carry a notebook. Write everything down. When you have an idea, write it down. When you meet someone new, write down everything you know about them. That way, you will know how much time they are worth. When you hear something interesting, write it down. Writing it down will make you act upon it. If you don't write it down you will forget it. That is a million-dollar lesson they don't teach you in business school!"*

Take a small notebook with you at all times. Titan ideas come to you when you least expect them, especially while relaxing, puttering, gardening, playing golf, showering, walking, driving, traveling and especially, while sleeping, so make sure you always have a small notebook on your nightstand to jot down your Titan ideas! As Richard Branson said, *"If you have a thought but don't write it down, by the next morning it may be gone forever."*

Here are some benefits of writing down your ideas on a notepad:

- **Boosts creativity**, as you will leave more room in your brain for more ideas to come.
- **Improves sleep**. If you get an idea during the night, write it down and go immediately back to sleep.
- **Increases your finances**. You are just one idea away from your Titan Life!

So write down your ideas, and most importantly, act upon them!

Titan Practice.

"It took me four years to paint like Raphael, but a life time to paint like a child."

– Picasso

Titan Practice is the "secret" behind every Titan. The journey to becoming a Titan is neither for the faint of heart nor for the impatient. Developing a Titan Skill takes struggle, sacrifice, patience and practice.

All Titans have in common 10,000 hours, which equals 10 years of practice. When you practice enough, you build muscle memory.

When practicing, this is the time for you to make mistakes. This is time for you to try things out. This is why many Titans refuse to permit the press to witness practice sessions, so they can practice with as little pressure as possible.

Former World Heavyweight Champion boxer, Jim Corbett, practiced throwing his left at his own image in the mirror over 10,000 times to prepare for his fight against the until-then undefeated champion John L. Sullivan.

Sir Harry Lauder, the famous Scottish actor and comedian, once admitted that he had practiced a certain routine over 10,000 times in private before ever giving the performance in public.

Everything should be arranged to make training and practice as relaxed and pressure-free as is humanly possible. The result is that *Titans go into the actual competition without appearing to have any nerves at all.* They trust the work they have done and depend on muscle memory to execute the various motions that they have learned.

Not All Practice Makes Perfect.

"It will take you at least a decade to achieve expertise, and you will need to invest that time wisely, by engaging in "deliberate practice" – practice that focuses on tasks beyond your current level of competence and comfort."

– K. Anders Ericsson

Not all practice makes perfect. *The quality of your practice determines the quality of your performance.*

When most people practice, they focus on the things they already know how to do. To practice like a Titan, you must *improve the skills you already have and work at eliminating your weaknesses.* This is the secret behind every Titan.

And of course, while everyone enjoys doing something you know how to do well, Titans allow themselves to 'suck' at the things they don't know how to do as well and work on them until they master them. This takes dedication, motivation, sacrifice and humility. Qualities that most people are not willing to put in.

As Sam Snead once said, *"It is only human nature to want to practice what you can already do well, since it's a hell of a lot less work and a hell of a lot more fun."*

How Long Should I Practice Each Day?

"Practice like you've never won. Play like you've never lost."
— Michael Jordan

The enormous concentration it takes to improve your strengths and eliminate your weaknesses limits the amount of time you can spend doing them.

The famous violinist Nathan Milstein wrote: *"Practice as much as you feel you can accomplish with concentration. Once when I became concerned because others around me practiced all day long, I asked [my mentor] Professor Auer how many hours I should practice, and he said, 'It really doesn't matter how long. If you practice with your fingers, no amount is enough. If you practice with your head, two hours is plenty.'"*

Practice as much as you feel you can accomplish with concentration. Most Titans, whether athletes, writers or musicians, engage in no more than four to five hours of Titan practice at a time.

Practice "Titan Incompetence."

"You only have to do a very few things right in your life so long as you don't do too many things wrong."
— Warren Buffett

Can you imagine doing your taxes, painting your house, fixing your plumbing yourself? I'm sure you could learn to do all of these activities, but the key to becoming a Titan is *focus*. *To become a Titan, you must be obsessed about your craft and practice day in and day out.* And this will take much energy and time from you. So you should practice "Titan Incompetence" to spend more time working on your Titan Skill.

Admit that you don't have time to do everything and let things go, or give it the minimum effort required. Obviously, there are some chores you can't ignore, but many of these can be simplified in such a way they don't interfere with your Titan Skill. *If something does not relate to your Titan Skill, practice "Titan Incompetence."* This is one secret to developing a Titan skill.

Strive For Excellence, Not Perfectionism.

"I am not a perfectionist, but I like to feel that things are done well. More important than that, I feel an endless need to learn, to improve, to evolve, not only to please the coach and the fans, but also to feel satisfied with myself."
– Cristiano Ronaldo

Perfectionism keeps us from completing the work. Please remember, the work will never be perfect! So we must strive for excellence!

Striving for excellence will motivate you; striving for perfection will disappoint you.

Mediocre people strive for good enough. Educated, middle-class people strive for an illusory perfectionism. Titans strive for excellence!

The difference between perfectionism and excellence is the ability to risk and even embrace failure. So the core difference is vulnerability.

When Pablo Casals was 95, a reporter asked him, *"Mr. Casals, you are 95 and the greatest cellist that ever lived. Why do you still practice six hours a day?"* Mr. Casals replied, *"Because I think I am making progress."*

Always strive for excellence. As Wayne Dyer said, *"It is never crowded along the extra mile."*

Make Decisions Promptly.

"Once I made a decision, I never thought about it again."
— Michael Jordan

While most people take a long time to make decisions, Titans make decisions promptly. While most people don't trust themselves or their abilities – so they believe they have to know every detail in advance – which you will never do – Titans see an opportunity and jump on it! As for most people? They are still preparing.

Stop asking for opinions and start proposing solutions: practice this in both your personal and professional lives. If you are asked, *'where shall we eat?'* Do not reflect it back with, *'Well, what do you want to eat?'* Offer a solution!

Get in the habit of making decisions promptly. Do not be afraid of making mistakes. Titans achieve their goals by going forward, making mistakes and immediately correcting course.

As Maxwell Maltz said, *"Skill learning of any kind is accomplished by trial and error, mentally correcting aim after an error, until a 'successful' motion, movement, or performance has been achieved. After that, further learning, and continued success is accomplished by forgetting the past errors, and remembering the successful response, so that it can be imitated."*

Do it Now!

"Whatever you do, or dream you can do, begin it.
Boldness has genius, power and magic in it."
— Johann Wolfgang von Goethe

The earlier you find your Titan Skill and work on refining it, the sooner you will become a Titan.

Wolfgang Amadeus Mozart started his musical tutelage before he was four years old. Rafael Nadal began playing tennis at age four. Leo Messi started playing football at five. Titans are not born. They are always made!

If you are an adult, and you haven't found your Titan Skill yet, do not despair! You can still become a Titan!

Henry Ford released the *Model T Ford* at age 45. Charles Darwin published *"On the Origin of the Species"* when he was 50. Ray Kroc started working with restaurant owners at age 53 and did not buy his first McDonald's until he was 59. Harland Sanders created Kentucky Fried Chicken at age 62. Anna Mary Robertson Moses started painting at age 78. And Harry Bernstein published his memoir at 96.

No matter your age, find your Titan Skill and start working on it, not tomorrow, but now! The more you delay working on your Titan Skill, the more painful it will be for you. Like Maya Angelou said, *"There is no greater agony than bearing an untold story inside you."*

Stop Making Excuses!

"The greater the difficulty, the more glory in surmounting it."
— Epictetus

Making excuses is one of the worst habits you can have. The reason most people fail is because they are great at making "rationalized" excuses. And why do they defend their excuses so strongly? Because they created them! As Napoleon Hill said, *"A man's alibi is the child of his own imagination. It is human nature to defend one's own brainchild."* Do you have a family to raise? Do you have a "regular" full-time job? Do you have any physical impediments? *While most people make excuses, Titans make things happen.*

John Grisham worked 70 hours per week at a law firm when he wrote his first novel. Leo Tolstoy had 13 kids, and, yet found time to write amazing books. And John Irving was dyslexic and needed more time than others to pick up his reading and writing skills at school, and yet, he became an award-winning writer!

The "perfect" circumstances to start working on your Titan Skill will never occur. Realize this and see what small action you could be taking today!

Are you too busy to practice your Titan Skill for four or five hours a day? No worries! Start from where you are. Use those "extra hours" of your day to build your Titan Skill. *The best time to do this is early in the morning or late at night, before and after your job and while the rest of the house sleeps.*

Two hours of daily Titan practice equal around 700 hours a year — around 7000 hours a decade! Think about what you could accomplish if you devoted two hours a day to Titan practice. You would become a Titan in no time! As George Eliot said, *"It's never too late to become who you might have been."*

Dream Big. Start Small.

"It is better to take many small steps in the right direction than to make a great leap forward only to stumble backward."
– Chinese proverb

Titans dream big, but start small. Ted Turner went to townhall lectures for free to practice for when he would get the chance to address the United Nations, which he eventually did!

Robert Collier stated, *"Success is the sum of small efforts, repeated day in and day out."*

And Richard Branson said, *"A big business starts small."*

Before you play in the "big leagues," you must play in the "smaller leagues." This concept can be applied to any field.

Weightlifters start with weights they can lift and gradually increase the weights over time. A good boxing manager starts a new boxer with easy opponents, and gradually matches him against more experienced fighters.

The idea is to start with an "opponent" over which you can succeed, and gradually take on more and more challenging "opponents."

Even after you develop a Titan Skill, it sometimes helps to "let go of the gas pedal" and practice with a feeling of ease. This is especially helpful when you reach a plateau in your progress. If this happens, go ahead and temporarily reduce the difficulty, whether it is reducing the weight on the bar, fighting an easier boxer or writing an article or short story instead of a book. *The idea is to build up Titan momentum again!*

Titan Performance.

"Train like you are No. 2, but compete like you are No. 1."
— Maurice Green

There's a story about a retired wrestler and his wife, who went to visit Floyd Mayweather before a fight. They just wanted to stop by to say hello and wish good luck with his fight. Upon entering the room, the couple found Mayweather relaxing and watching TV. The couple and Mayweather were chatting for a while, when the retired wrestler said, *"Alright, Floyd, we'll get going here, so you can get ready for your fight."* Mayweather replied, *"No worries, man! Relax! Have another drink."* They kept chatting and enjoying some more refreshments. A few more minutes went by, and the retired wrestler signaled to his wife, and they both stood up. *"Now, we'd better get going, so you can prepare for your fight,"* said the retired wrestler. To which Mayweather replied: *"Dude, relax! Preparation was done months ago. If I'm not ready by now, there's not much I can do at this point. So I must trust the preparation I've done."*

As a Titan, you must practice extremely hard, but then, when it's competition day, you must trust the work you have done. Adding unnecessary nerves and anxiety on competition day will not help you! Sure, every Titan feels some pressure on competition day, but now you must trust your preparation and use that pressure as an opportunity to rise to the occasion! Trust that your years of training will now take over, and you will almost be on autopilot! So relax by focusing on the breathing and on being in the present, and simply let your Titan come out!

Another Titan strategy is to *always mentally downsize the importance of the event, no matter how "important" the event may be.* You will perform much better!

And the final Titan strategy is to *use visualization and affirmations* (as explained in the *Titan Mind* chapter), to evoke the "winning feeling." As Dr. Maxwell Maltz said, *"When you feel successful and self-confident, you will act successfully."* When the winning feeling is strong, you can literally do no wrong!

Promote Your Titan Value.

"Early to bed, early to rise, work like hell, and advertise."
— *Ted Turner*

While most people think negatively about selling and promoting, Titans will promote themselves and their value. In fact, Titans are excellent promoters!

Titans will promote their products, their services and their idea with passion and enthusiasm. They are skilled at packaging their value in a way that's extremely attractive.

To be a Titan, you must inherently have followers and supporters, which means that you must be adept at selling, inspiring, and motivating people to buy into your Titan Vision. How else will you be able to create a large income in your business if you are not willing to let people know that you, your product or service exist? And if you think this "only applies to businesspeople," think twice! Nelson Mandela, Mother Teresa and the Dalai Lama had no qualms about promoting their causes and asking for money for their causes!

If you have a problem with promotion, it only means that either you don't fully believe in your product or you don't fully believe in yourself.

If you believe that you have something special that can bring Titan value to the world, it is your duty, as a Titan, to let as many people as possible know about it. This way, not only will you be able to help people, but also you will become rich!

Failure Is The Price Titans Pay.

"I don't believe in failure. I believe failure is just information.
It is information and opportunity to change your course."
– Oprah Winfrey

Success is not possible without failure. Titans become so because they fail the most. While most people see failure as failure, Titans see it as a valuable database to see what's not working and to improve their Titan Skill.

Edison failed over 10,000 times before perfecting the incandescent electric light bulb. When he was asked about what he thought of "having failed over 10,000 times," he simply replied, *"I have not failed 10,000 times. I have successfully discovered 10,000 ways to not make electricity."*

Lord Sebastian Coe stated, *"Winning is built on a robust diet of defeat."*

Henry Ford said, *"Failure is simply the opportunity to begin again, this time more intelligently."*

Richard Branson stated, *"You don't learn to walk by following rules. You learn by doing, and falling over, and it's because you fall over that you learn to save yourself from falling over."*

And JK Rowling said, *"It is impossible to live without failing at something, unless you live so cautiously that you might as well not have lived at all – in which case, you fail by default."*
Titans are used to failing. This is why Titans never take things for granted because they've lived that other life and have had to wade through seas of pain. *There's a certain humility and empathetic nature that's instilled in the hearts of Titans, who had to endure a lot of failure before tasting the sweet taste of victory.*
We, humans, always learn more by the setbacks than by what goes well. So don't worry if you fail once, twice or 10,000 times! What matters is that you embrace failure and keep pressing through. *You are only successful at the last attempt!*

Dealing With Criticism.

"To avoid criticism say nothing, do nothing, be nothing."
– Aristotle

When you become a Titan, when you know about your field more than anybody else, people will feel threatened. Why do they feel like this? *Because you show them possibility, and this makes them feel small.* Because they could also become Titans, but they would have to accept responsibility for their own lives and they would have to change. And people don't like that! So the defense mechanism of these people is criticizing you.
In 1879, a journalist from the *New York Daily Graphic* wrote this about Thomas Edison, *"Day after day, week after week, and month after month passes, and Mr. Edison does not illumine Menlo Park with his electric light. The belief*

has become rather general in this country and in England that for once, the great inventor has miscalculated his inventive resources and utterly failed."

All Titans were initially misunderstood. They were called "strange" and "crazy." They were criticized, ridiculed and loathed before they were understood and revered. As Gandhi said, *"First they ignore you, then they laugh at you, then they fight you, then you win."*

Keep marching to the melody that your ears alone can hear. Don't listen to the critics! Don't empower them by answering their critiques! Everyone has an opinion. To be loved by many, you will be loathed by many others. *You can change the world, or you can worry about criticism, but you can't do both.*

The very nature of being a Titan is that you will challenge the status quo. It means you will think and speak in a way that most people are not willing to accept. This is why you will be criticized. *If you are not criticized a lot, if you are not laughed at often, it means you are dreaming small.*

Dealing With Rejection.

"I am thankful for all of those who said 'no' to me. It's because of them I'm doing it myself."
                                                    – Albert Einstein

While most people are discouraged and defeated when someone tells them, *"You can't do it!,"* Titans take this as fuel for them to aggressively rise to the occasion and become determined to prove this person wrong.

So stop listening to the nay-sayers, or better yet, "listen" to them and prove them wrong! You, your family and the world will thank you for it!

Remain A Titan.

"Stay hungry. Stay foolish."

– *Steve Jobs*

At your point of most success, you are the most vulnerable because nothing fails like success!

When you become a Titan, it is very easy to fall in love with your success. The moment you feel entitled to your success is the beginning of the end. Never take your success for granted! It could all be gone tomorrow! As Bill Gates said, *"Success is a lousy teacher. It seduces smart people into thinking they can't lose."*

Amancio Ortega eats lunch with his employees in the company cafeteria every day, so he doesn't get a sense of entitlement. Russian tennis players work out at decrepit gym facilities, so they stay hungry. And Maya Angelou wrote at run-down motels.

Stay hungry, keep improving, and, as Mark Cuban said, *"Work as though someone was working 24 hours a day to take it all away from you."*

T

TITAN TEAM

"The climb upwards will be easier
if you take others along with you."

– Napoleon Hill

Are you tired of not getting the results you know in your heart you should be getting? If you are doing everything else well, the chances are that you're trying to do it all solo.

Many entrepreneurs, artists, and athletes fail to understand that *to get Titan results, you must surround yourself by a Titan Team.*

Any sports team relies more on harmonious coordination of effort than individual skill. Any Titan achievement is always the result of a collaborative effort.

How can you scale up your business if you do everything yourself? As much as you would like to do everything yourself, if you want to achieve Titan things in life, you will need a Titan Team!

The Myth Of The Lone Titan.

"Getting the right people in the right roles in support of your goal
is the key to succeeding at whatever you choose to accomplish."
– Ray Dalio

Most people have romantic notions about Titans. We think of them as geniuses who spend a long time working in their labs alone until they finally have their eureka moment and solve the world's problems. But most people don't realize these Titans are never alone! They all have Titan Teams behind them.

Thomas Edison had a team of 14 people. His name is on 10,000 patents. He did not invent a single thing by himself. He marshaled the people together.

Andrew Carnegie stated, *"Teamwork is the ability to work together toward a common vision. The ability to direct individual accomplishments toward organizational objectives. It is the fuel that allows common people to attain uncommon results."*

And Steve Jobs said, *"I've never created anything. All I did was noticed patterns and put people together to finish projects."*

The "lone Titan" is a myth! And until you realize that becoming a Titan requires a Titan Team, you will never get there, at least, not as fast as you could helped by a Titan Team!

Building Your Titan Team.

"It doesn't make sense to hire smart people and tell them what to do; we hire smart people so they can tell us what to do."
– Steve Jobs

You can't build a Titan company, career or project if you are surrounded by mediocre team members.

See yourself as a Titan and surround yourself with a team of people that keeps you physically, psychologically, mentally, spiritually and professionally at your best. Hire the best, and then let them do what they know!

Cristiano Ronaldo, as a young player for Manchester United, hired a nutritionist, a physician, a personal physio and a chef. Here's how ex-footballer and ex-teammate Rio Ferdinand described it: *"They came and lived in his house more or less, he lived a couple of doors up from me. Going into his house was like a carnival, people walking around, I used to think 'wow, what's going on here?' But he invested in himself to become the best in the world and he left Manchester United as the best player in the world."*

Titans invest in surrounding themselves with a Titan Team. You might think, *'Yes, but these people have money. I can't afford it."* First, stop saying, *"I can't afford it,"* in case you end up believing it! Instead, ask yourself *"how could I afford it?"* And second, while I understand you might – currently! – not have the same financial resources as a football star, start from where you are! What team members can you afford? Start with them. And as you become more Titan, the quality of your team members will become more Titan as well!

Please remember, *building a Titan Team is not an expense, but an investment.* Always focus on value, not on price.

Managing Your Titan Team.

"Lead from the back, and let others believe they are in front."
– Nelson Mandela

You, as the Titan, must set the tone for excellence at which you and your team will be playing. For this, you must work and practice even when your team is sleeping or resting! If you set this Titan level of excellence, your team will follow your footsteps.

Your team will model your behavior. As the leader of the team, your job is to inspire them with your *Titanness* – I know, I just made up this word! –, praise them and encourage them. This forges Titans!

And don't hesitate to fire a team member playing at a mediocre level. Mediocrity, the same as excellence, spreads quickly to the rest of the team. Even one team member playing average will destroy your Titan Team!

Titan Coaches & Titan Mentors.

*"A mentor is someone who allows you to
see the hope inside yourself."*

– *Oprah Winfrey*

Titans are devoted students who look for devoted coaches and mentors.

Initially, most Titans are taught by local coaches: Wolfgang Amadeus Mozart was under his father's tutelage. Leo Messi was trained by his father. And Rafael Nadal was trained by his uncle.

But as their level of expertise increases, Titans study with more advanced coaches. Eventually, *all Titans work with coaches who are Titans themselves.*

Developing a Titan requires coaches capable of giving constructive, even painful, feedback, who are always challenging them and driving them to higher levels of performance and who can identify the aspects of your performance to be improved.

A Titan Coach will not only guide you through your Titan practice but will also help you to learn how to coach yourself. As your expertise increases, *your coach will help you become more and more independent so you can have an awareness of what needs to be improved.*

Make no mistake, if you want to accelerate your learning process, put coaches and mentors in your life. And in the process, you will become a mentor or coach to others!

Titan tip: Email a mentor. If you write them from your heart, offering to work for them for free, you'd be surprised how many mentors might say yes.

Self-Coaching.

"Many who are self-taught far excel the doctors, masters, and bachelors of the most renowned universities."
– Ludwig von Mises

If you – currently! – cannot afford or do not have access to coaches or mentors, then, self-coaching is how to go!

Self-coaching can be done in any field. As they say, *"Where there's a will, there's a way!"*

Many Titans throughout history have been self-taught: Christopher Columbus, Leonardo Da Vinci, Galileo Galilei, Benjamin Franklin, Abraham Lincoln, Karl Marx, Mark Twain, Thomas Alva Edison, Nikola Tesla, Henry Ford, Frank Lloyd Wright, the Wright Brothers, Henry Miller, Ernest Hemingway, Frida Kahlo, Jose Saramago, Jimi Hendrix, Steven Spielberg, Bruce Springsteen, Steve Jobs, Quentin Tarantino, the list goes on!

Benjamin Franklin provides one of the best examples of self-coaching. When he wanted to learn to write eloquently and persuasively, he studied his favorite articles from a popular British publication, *The Spectator*. Days after he'd read an article he particularly enjoyed, he would try to reconstruct it from memory in his own words. Then he would compare it with the original, so he could make corrections.

We learn just about everything from modeling. Picasso started by reproducing the paintings of previous Titans. Imitating your Titan role models is like using training wheels on a child's bicycle; they help you get going, but once you find your own rhythm and balance, you fly faster and farther without leaning on them.

If you are going to be self-taught, read the biographies of the Titans you admire. Study their lives and get inspired by their achievements. Study their technique. Copy them. Then, develop your own Titan style!

Your Titanmind Group.

"The coordination of knowledge and effort between two or more people who work towards a definite purpose in a spirit of harmony... no two minds ever come together without thereby creating a third, invisible intangible force, which may be likened to a third mind."

– Napoleon Hill

A Titanmind group is one of the most powerful tools ever used by Titans – whether the world's richest industrialists from the early 20th century or today's modern Titans of business.

Henry Ford, Thomas Edison, Alexander Graham Bell, Theodore Roosevelt, John D. Rockefeller, Charles M. Schwab, Andrew Carnegie all attributed their success to these types of groups.

Your Titanmind group differs from your Titan Team. It is like *a board of advisors to help you become Titan in your field and in life*. It brings together people from different industries and professions, so you get different perspectives on the same subject and, equally or more importantly, get access to a network of people you normally wouldn't have access to.

By getting the perspective, knowledge, experience and resources of others in the group, not only will you be able to expand your view of the world, but also you will advance your Titan goals more quickly.

Can you imagine having a group of advisors who meet regularly for problem-solving, brainstorming, networking, encouraging and motivating each other, and holding each other accountable for achieving their goals, whether professional or personal?

Running Your Titanmind Group.

"Never doubt that a small group of thoughtful, committed
citizens can change the world. Indeed, it is the
only thing that ever has."

– Margaret Mead

A Titanmind group comes together regularly – weekly, biweekly, or monthly – to share ideas, thoughts, information, feedback, contacts and resources.

The ideal size of your Titanmind group is between six and eight people. If your Titanmind group is smaller, it loses its dynamics. And if it's bigger, it's harder to manage and harder for all members to commit frequently.

J. Richard Hackman, professor of Social and Organizational Psychology at Harvard University, said, *"Big teams usually wind up just wasting everybody's time."*

And Jeff Bezos said, *"If you can't feed a team with two pizzas, it's too large."*

A Titanmind group can focus on business issues, personal issues or both. But for a Titanmind group to be effective, people must be comfortable enough with each other to speak their mind.

Make sure that the members of the Titanmind group are either at your "level" or, ideally, "above." You need people who will elevate you to become a Titan!

Contrary to regular team meetings where the group tends to be dominated by one or two people, a Titanmind group must allow each member to participate equally. Your mission is not to lead the group – they are all leaders after all!–, but to *keep harmony among the members of the group.* This way, the entire group will be benefited.

Do you all live in different cities or countries? That's no excuse! Thanks to technology, Titanmind groups are easier than ever!

While you must always do the work of becoming a Titan, a Titanmind group can – and will! – speed up your Titan results.

Titan tip: Who would form your ideal Titanmind group? Think Richard Branson, Bill Gates, Warren Buffett, Jeff Bezos, the Dalai Lama, Arnold Schwarzenegger. What would be the closest you could get access to now?

T

TITAN ENVIRONMENT

"Surround yourself with those who only lift you higher."
– Oprah Winfrey

A Titan Environment is the "invisible hand" that will help you build your Titan Life.

The environment is one of the most overlooked, yet crucial contributing factors to building the life you want. This includes, but is not limited to, the type of home, office, people, books, media that surround you daily. *Your environment is the clearest indicator of who you are and who you're becoming.*

Habits grow out of the environment. *Our environment drives our good behaviors and our bad ones.* If your environment is not conducive to you becoming a Titan, your odds of success are very low. On the flip side, creating a Titan Environment accelerates your results and makes winning easier.

Changing yourself, both personally and professionally, begins with changing your environment. Set up your surroundings in such a way that making Titan decisions comes easily without having to "stay motivated." *Surround yourself by an environment where failure is not an option!*

Think about your environment (home, office, people,…). Is it conducive to you becoming a Titan? Simple changes to your environment can make a Titan difference. For example, if you want to practice playing the violin, place it in the middle of your living room. To eat healthier food, you should stock up with healthier options. If your neighborhood is filled with negativity, listen to positive audiobooks when walking around it.

So look around yourself and see how you can make your environment more conducive to you becoming a Titan.

Are You Doomed By Your Environment?

"The soul is stronger than its surroundings."
– *William James*

Whether we like it or not, our minds are easily swayed by external forces. *We are products of our environment.*

If you come from a "tough neighborhood," where poverty and drugs are part of daily life, understand that your chances of success are quite low. This is why most people who come from these types of neighborhoods end up not doing well in life. But do not despair!

There are many Titans who also came from tough neighborhoods or had difficult initial circumstances, and they used these as fuel for them to realize the type of life they did not want to have in the future. Here are some examples: Sheldon Adelson, Larry Ellison, Oprah Winfrey, Stephen King, Ralph Lauren, J.K. Rowling, Howard Schultz, Jay-Z, Jennifer Lopez, Leonardo Di Caprio among many others. These Titans, whether consciously or unconsciously, created a world of their own making, while living in the very real world of negativity that surrounded them.

If your environment is not the best, no worries! Use this as fertilizer for you to become a Titan! Create your own bubble: read biographies, listen to audiobooks, use visualization, isolate yourself from the world around you and work like a Titan!

Your Titan Circle.

"A man only learns in two ways: one by reading,
and the other by association with smarter people."
– Will Rogers

How much would your finances improve if you were friends with Warren Buffett? How much better your fitness would be if you were friends with Arnold Schwarzenegger? And how much more spiritual you would become if you were friends with the Dalai Lama? You guessed it. Much better! *Because your associations determine the life you have.*

If you look at the five people you spend most of your time with, your weight, values and salary is an average of their weight, values and salaries. As they say, *"Birds of a feather, flock together."*

Titans don't simply join the country club to play golf; they join to connect with other Titans.

Your Titan Circle is a greater predictor of your performance than your genes. Your life reflects the influences you are exposing your mind to. You become your associations. This is due to a biological mechanism in our brain called *mirror neuron system*, through which our brains practice doing actions we merely observe in others. Your behavior models the behavior of those you spend most of your time with.

A study at Dartmouth College by economist Bruce Sacerdote found that students who weren't achieving great grades raised them noticeably simply by finding roommates doing well. The researcher wrote, *"The students appeared to infect each other with good habits that caused better grades."*

If you want to become a Titan, associate with Titans! You might be thinking, *"Sure... but Titans don't want to associate with me."* And you're probably right since Titans are very careful with whom they spend their time. So how do you associate with Titans? There are two ways:

1. **Through reading their autobiographies,** so you expose your mind to the way Titans think and operate.
2. **Through becoming a Titan in your field.** And, as you become more Titan in your field, Titans will want to associate with you.

Stay Away From Toxic People.

"Keep away from people who try to belittle your ambitions. Small people always do that, but the really great make you feel that you, too, can become great."

– Mark Twain

Titans know that other people's energies and emotions could potentially influence them.

Your subconscious mind is constantly absorbing information, drawing conclusions and forming beliefs based on that information. *If your daily environment is filled with negativity, your subconscious mind is absorbing those messages daily.*

Were a friend or family member to throw garbage into your house, you would fight with them and would stop spending time with them. But then, when a friend or family member throws "garbage" into your mind, you don't fight them and, often, you continue spending time with them!

To have a Titan Life, you must completely delete or, at least, limit – with "well-intended" parents or siblings – the negativity you expose yourself to daily. Stay away from people who are negative, selfish, energy vampires, crazy-makers, cynics, gossipers, arrogant, victims and complainers. *And surround yourself with people who talk about possibility, who are ambitious, who discuss ideas and talk about dreams, who take care of themselves, who love traveling.* This will make you want to do something about your life too!

Extricate yourself from negative environments and build an environment of people who only see greatness in you, and who support you on this journey to becoming a Titan!

I'm not suggesting that you should be rude to people and only spend time with Titans. But there are people to spend 5 minutes with, people to have dinner with, people to spend a weekend with, and people to be with daily. The problem is when you don't know the difference and you spend a weekend with someone who is a 5-minute person!

Live In Possibility-Land.

"I dwell in possibility…"
– Emily Dickinson

For many years, runners from around the world strove to run a mile under 4 minutes. This was the "Holy Grail" of athletic achievement, and it became as much a psychological barrier as a physical one. Whether consciously or unconsciously, athletes believed it was "impossible" to achieve this. This belief was backed by the opinions of coaches and experts of the time. So the four-minute barrier stood for decades!

Then, in 1954, an outlier, Roger Bannister, a full-time student not part of the system in the sense he had no coaches and who devised his own system for preparing to race, suddenly busted through the four-minute barrier with a time of three minutes, fifty-nine and four-tenths of a second! When Bannister broke the mark, even his rivals breathed a sigh of relief. *"Finally!"*

What happened next? Only 46 days after Bannister's feat, John Landy broke the barrier again, and with a time of 3 minutes 58 seconds. And then, just a year later, three more runners broke the four-minute barrier in a single race! Over the last half-century, more than a thousand runners have conquered a barrier once considered "impossible."

This is why it's important that you surround yourself, whether directly or through their autobiographies, with people who show you possibility!

Titan Work Environment.

"People are offended when you repeatedly turn down their invitations. But I decided that the indispensable relationship in my life was with my readers."

– Haruki Murakami

Many Titans seem reclusive, but what they are really doing is protecting the time that brings them happiness, sometimes at the expense of other aspects of their lives. *Titans know how important it is to protect their space, control their environment and be free of distractions if they want to produce Titan level of work.*

Thomas Edison had his Menlo Park lab. Einstein had his Princeton University office. And Kanye West rented a house in Hawaii and "imported" his favorite producers and artists to work on one of his albums.

You must create your own "Menlo Park" to develop your Titan Skill. It could be a room in your home, a park, the public library, a coffee-shop, your own garage. (Garages are where companies such as Harley Davidson, Microsoft, Disney, Amazon, HP, Mattel, Google and Apple all started!) When you go into your Titan Work Environment, eliminate distractions. Turn off your mobile phone – or put it on "Do not disturb." (You can set it up to allow calls from your family in case of emergency.) Be unreachable! *Most people are devoted to distractions. Titans are devoted to results.*

Next, really pour yourself into whatever you are doing until you forget the outside world! This is called *transient hypofrontality.* Some people call it "flow." Others call it "being in the zone." Whatever you call it, get to that state. Only then, will you be able to come up with your Titan ideas and do your Titan work!

A Titan tool to experience *transient hypofrontality* is music. This is why many Titans, such as writers, painters and professional athletes, listen to music before – or while – working on their Titan Skill.

Tennis player Rafael Nadal is a great example of him "bringing" his Titan Work Environment to whatever tennis court he is playing at. From fiddling with his hair and shirt before every serve to the way he organizes his water bottles, these "quirks" to some, make Nadal "get in the zone", so he can play his Titan tennis!

Other Tips For Creating A Titan Work Environment.

- **Organize** your workspace to minimize visual distractions.
- **Use your flight-time as Titan time.** If you're stuck on a plane for hours, use this time to develop your Titan Skill.
- **Live in – or rent – a cabin** in the middle of nowhere. Work on your craft, spend time with your family, spend time in nature, read, eat and sleep.

Titan Hotbeds.

"The greatest education in the world is watching the masters at work."

– Michael Jackson

Have you ever wondered why the best footballers play in Europe, the best film directors work in Hollywood and some of the best chefs live in Spain? No, it's not their genes. It's the environment!

When you are constantly surrounded by an environment of Titans of your field, your skill will be infused by the way these Titans operate. You will accelerate your learning simply by watching!

Leonardo Da Vinci's family moved to Florence when Leonardo was a teenager. Florence was the center of Humanist thought and culture; a city buzzing with creative ideas and a popular hub for talented artists. Had he not moved to Florence, Leonardo might not have become Leonardo Da Vinci!

So what is the Titan Hotbed of your field? Consider moving there!

A Titan Home Environment.

*"A home should be a stockade, a refuge from the
flaming arrows of anxiety, tension and worry."*
— *Wilfred Peterson*

Titans make sure that their homes are their "sanctuaries."
Our homes are where we spend most of our time. This is
why *we must create a Titan Home Environment for us to
thrive, love, enjoy and rest.*
A peaceful life in the countryside seems pretty common
among Titans and those who have watched a century pass.
Use the city for business and the countryside for living.
A Titan home should be a minimalist, almost zen-like
home, where rooms are kept clean and uncluttered. *Your
visual environment affects your state of mind.* Messy homes
create messy minds. This is why it's important to keep your
home well organized! Here are some benefits of having a
Titan Home Environment:

- **Reduces stress** and anxiety.
- **Improves mental** stability.
- Increases **focus and productivity**.
- Improves **sleep**.
- You are more likely to **make healthier food choices**.

Aside from keeping your home tidy and clean, use green
cleaning products around the house. What's the point of
keeping a tidy and clean house if it's full of chemicals?

Become A Minimalist.

"Simplicity is the ultimate sophistication."
— *Leonardo Da Vinci*

One secret of Titans is simplicity. If you think about it, *what makes a masterpiece is its simplicity.*

Instead of focusing on many things, focus on just a few: your skill, your family, your health, your friends, your legacy,... Strip away from complexity. It is not about what you add into, but what you take out. Like Michelangelo said referring to his masterpiece *David, "The sculpture was already complete within the marble block before I started my work. It was already there. I just had to chisel away what didn't belong to David."*

What are your Titan 5 for Life? Master these! Build your life around your Titan 5 for Life. What you dwell on determines your destiny. Chisel away everything that doesn't belong to your Titan Life. Always ask yourself, *Will this simplify my life?*

Other Titan Tips For Simplifying Your Life.

- **Travel light.** Carry around less stuff.
- Hire a **virtual assistant.**
- **Live closer to work.** Could you work from home?
- **Don't watch TV.** It's usually mindless. There are some great shows and movies, but most TV is mindless. As a Titan, most people's recreations don't recreate you.
- **Check your email once or twice a day** at specific times.
- **Be careful what you listen to on the radio!**
- **Cultivate selective ignorance.** Don't watch the news unless your job depends on daily news. The most important news, you will hear about anyway! All those wars, hunger, car accidents, murders only

debilitate your immune system, creativity and energy levels. (Reading the news once a week to know what's going in the world is enough.)

- **Stop your addiction to social media and videogames.** It's preventing you from living your Titan Life!
- **Focus on quality, not quantity!** Instead of having fifteen pairs of 'OK' shoes in your closet, have a couple of great ones! Instead of buying tons of junk foods, buy less, but high quality foods! Instead of having twenty "friends," have one or two Titan friends! Instead of vacationing at 3-star hotels for a week, go to a 5-star hotel for one or two nights! Instead of going to a mediocre restaurant, go to the best restaurant in town and order a cup of tea. Feel the sophistication! Instead of drinking cheap wine every day, drink excellent wine once a week! A Titan Life is about surrounding yourself by Titan things. Always quality over quantity!

T

TITAN FINANCES

"Money is a terrible master, but an excellent servant."
– P.T. Barnum

Money might not buy you happiness, but it sure helps you become happier. Here is the thing, you could be a very spiritual person, but if you don't have the financial means to pay for your rent and groceries, your spirituality will go out the window in stress and anxiety.

Money is an essential commodity that helps you run your life. Money is a great facilitator.

Titans tend to live longer and better quality lives than people who live in poverty. The reason behind it is simple: you can live in better areas with better air quality, you can afford better quality foods, you live less stressed lives (at least, in terms of financial stress). If you have kids, money will provide them with access to better schools, better food and better health care (if you come from a country with no universal health care). Your kids will have a better start in life!

With money, you can also take your family on great vacations around the world; you can live Titan experiences; you can drive safer cars; you can wear nicer clothes; you can afford to have a maid, so you can enjoy more time with your family.

Money is important because it enables you to have more control and freedom over your life. You don't live life paycheck to paycheck. It's about working wherever and whenever you want! As Ralph Waldo Emerson said, *"The desire of gold is not for gold. It is for the means of freedom and benefit."*

Another great reason – if not the greatest reason – to have Titan Finances is so you can affect the community. Look at Oprah Winfrey and the numerous projects she donates money to, like her school in South Africa. *The more money you make, the larger the impact you can make in society.*

And you know what's most important about making tons of money? *The Titan you become, your own personal growth.* Because money is always a byproduct of your level of excellence at what you do. As Henry David Thoreau said, *"What you get by achieving your goals is not as important as what you become by achieving your goals."*

Money Is A State Of Mind.

"I have about concluded that wealth is a state of mind, and that anyone can acquire a wealthy state of mind by thinking rich thoughts."
– Andrew Young

Financial wealth, like other types of wealth, is a state of mind. It's not about having wealth; *it's about having the power to produce wealth.* It's intrinsic!

When you compare the thoughts, beliefs, and philosophies about money between the Titans and most people, the differences are as extreme as they are numerous. *But they all come down to a different state of mind regarding money.*

While most people believe that money doesn't grow on trees, Titans believe that money does actually grow on trees; and the "trees" are ideas that solve human problems. Like

William Feather said, *"Wealth flows from energy and ideas."* And the more problems you solve, the more money you make! Like Napoleon Hill said, *"Ideas can be transmuted into cash through the power of definite purpose, plus definite plans."*

While most people believe that money is scarce and difficult to earn, Titans believe that money is abundant and easy to earn. While most people play it safe with money, Titans take "calculated" risks with it. While most people believe that to make more money you must work longer hours, Titans believe in working smarter. While most people say, *"I can't afford it,"* Titans say *"How can I afford it?"* While most people spend money they don't have, Titans save and invest the money they have. While most people are consumers, Titans are makers. While most people buy "toys," Titans buy sources of passive income that will generate money for them to buy "toys." While most people work for a salary, Titans work for free. While most people resent wealthy people, Titans admire other wealthy people. While most people "want" or "wish" to be rich, *Titans are committed to being rich.*

Your Attitude Towards Money.

"Run for your life from any man who tells you that money is evil. That sentence is the leper's bell of an approaching looter."

– Ayn Rand

Many people have an issue with money. They think that money is evil, and that wealthy people are lucky or dishonest. This "programming" goes back to the bible where it states that *"love of money is the root of all evil."*

Money is not good or evil. It simply magnifies who you are deep down. If you like to help, if you have great amounts of money, you can help many people! But if you don't care about others, with great amounts of money, you will become even more selfish and arrogant. *Money simply magnifies who you are.*

If your motivation for acquiring money comes from fear, anger or greed, your money will never bring you happiness. But if your motivation for acquiring money comes from wanting financial security, freedom, control over your life and making a difference in people's lives, then money will bring you much happiness.

Most people have been programmed to believe that they don't have the right, nor are they good enough to ask for financial prosperity beyond their basic needs. They ask, *"Who am I to want to become a millionaire?"* Titans believe that they are as good as any and that they deserve to be rich. They ask, *"Why not me if they can do it?"*

Never feel bad about wanting to have more money and never let others make you feel guilty about wanting to have more money. You are meant to live a life of abundance. You are meant to live a Titan Life!

If you want to be rich, everything starts by changing your attitude towards money.

Financial Freedom.

"Wealth is the ability to fully experience life."
– Henry David Thoreau

How much money does it take to become financially free? Is it $1,000.000? 1,000,000,000? None of the above! You become financially free the minute *your monthly passive income is higher than your monthly expenses.*

So if you want to become financially free, you must create sources of passive income. As you probably noticed, I didn't say "source," but "sources." Why? Because *depending on only one source of income is way too risky.* So we must create multiple streams of passive income. As Warren Buffett said, *"Never depend on single income. Make investment to create a second source."*

Passive Income Sources.

"If you don't find a way to make money while you sleep, you will work until you die."
— *Warren Buffett*

Here are some Titan Passive Income sources:
- **Financial instruments**: stocks, bonds, T-bills, mutual funds, owning mortgages.
- **Real Estate**: residential and commercial properties.
- **Online businesses on *Amazon FBA*.** Yes, Amazon will take a percentage, but they will take care of everything for you!
- **Royalties** from books, music, movies, software.
- Mobile **apps**.
- **Storage** units.
- **Parking** lots.
- Automatic **car-washes**.
- **ATM** machines.
- **Vending** machines.
- **Affiliate** marketing.
- Become a **franchisor**.
- **Online blog**.
- **Membership** website.

All the above businesses can be set up in such a way they will make money for you while you sleep!

Net worth Vs. Salary.

"It's not how much money you make, but how much money you keep, how hard it works for you, and how many generations you keep it for."
— *Robert Kiyosaki*

Most people believe that their wealth is their salary. *Your wealth is your total net worth.* It is the part of your balance sheet considered *equity.* Your assets minus your liabilities.

While most people focus on getting a higher salary, Titans focus on increasing their net worth. While most people make money from their salaries, Titans make money from their profits. *To get rich, you will need to be paid based on results.*

Always focus on building your net worth. Here are some Titan strategies to increase your net worth:

Your Income Is A Byproduct Of Your Excellence.

"Never forget: the secret of creating riches for oneself is to create them for others."
— *John Templeton*

Your income will always be a byproduct of your excellence at what you do. This is why if you want to increase your income, focus on bringing more value to the market place. Like Bernard Arnault said, *"Money is just a consequence. I always say to my team, 'Don't worry too much about profitability. If you do your job well, the profitability will come.'."*

The reason the person flipping hamburgers is earning minimum wage is that anyone can do that. But the reason Titans make so much money is that very few people can do what they do in their respective fields. They bring much more value to the market place! I'm not saying that flipping burgers is better or worse than being a Titan, but while the marketplace will pay $1 for a burger, *the same market place will pay thousands or millions of dollars to see a Titan perform.* And the reason Titans can bring that Titan Value is that they went through the process of putting in thousands of hours of practice into their Titan Skill, so they became extremely valuable to society.

This reminds me of the story about a woman who approached Picasso in a restaurant, and asked him to scribble something on a napkin. In response, Picasso pulled out a charcoal pencil from his pocket and swiftly sketched an image of a goat. The woman reached out to collect the napkin, but Picasso withheld it. *"That will be $100,000,"* said Picasso. The woman, outraged, said, *"$100,000? It took you less than thirty seconds to draw that!* Picasso replied, *"No, my dear, it took me forty years of my life to be able to draw that in thirty seconds."*

So if you want to increase your income, become more valuable to the market place. It's as simple as that!

Live With 50% Of Your Income.

"The habit of saving is itself an education; it fosters every virtue, teaches self-denial, cultivates the sense of order, trains to forethought, and so broadens the mind."

– T. T. Munger

Every dollar you save is a "seed" that can be planted to earn a hundred more dollars, which can then be replanted to earn a thousand more dollars, which can then be replanted to earn millions! While most people save money if they have anything left, Titans save money first, and then, spend whatever money they have left. *Live with 50% of your income, so you can save the other 50%.* Develop the habit of saving fifty cents of every dollar earned. Make a game out of it! If you currently can't save 50% of your income, start with 25%! Like Jeff Bezos said, *"I think frugality drives innovation, just like other constraints do. One of the only ways to get out of a tight box is to invent your way out."* Invent your way out to save 50% of your income!

One thing that most people have problems with is budgeting. *Spend according to the budget you have, not according to the lifestyle you think you should be living.* For this, the first thing we must do is to know our budget. How else are you going to save 50% of your income if you don't know where your money is going? List your income and your monthly expenses (estimate in round numbers). Look for places to cut or reduce expenses:

- **Pay off your credit card debt.** Credit card interests are financially killing you! First, pay off the credit cards with the highest interest rates. Once you pay off your first credit card, just move down the list until they are all paid off.
- **Eat at home or pack your sandwich.** The more you cook, the healthier and wealthier you will become!
- Instead of going to the movies, **take a walk through your neighborhood** and discover new places.

- **Cut your cable TV**, which is very expensive, find cheaper alternatives such as *Netflix* or *Amazon Prime.*
- **Buy in bulk and on sale.** It's your favorite coffee on sale? Buy a two-year supply!
- **Reduce energy costs:** take shorter showers (not fewer!), wash your clothes in cold tap water, install dimmer switches and LED lightbulbs.
- **Save money on your mobile phone service** by getting rid of extras like costly data plans, phone insurance and unnecessary warranties. And don't be afraid to ask for additional discounts or completely switch your provider!
- **DIY (Do It Yourself) everything.** If you need to fix something in the house, buy the materials yourself and watch a tutorial on YouTube. If you still need help, ask a friend or family member.
- **Negotiate with cash.** If someone is selling goods or services to you, offer them cash and ask them for a discount. They will take the cash!
- **Travel cheaper.** Purchase plane tickets far in advance (three months or more), and aim for both departure and return between Tuesday and Thursday. Also, consider buying one ticket to an international hub, and then an ongoing ticket with a cheap local airline.

If you do the above, you will see you can save more money each month!

Aim to save six months of expenses and put it into a savings account. By doing this, you will have the peace of mind that if something goes wrong – you get fired or you decide to do something else – you will have the financial means to be covered for the next six months!

Pay Yourself First... If It Makes Financial Sense!

" 'A part of all I earn is mine to keep.' Say it in the morning when you first arise. Say it at noon. Say it at night. Say it each hour of every day. Say it to yourself until the words stand out like letters of fire across the sky."
– George S. Clason

"Pay yourself first" is a practice recommended by many Titans. It basically states that instead of paying your debtors first, pay yourself 10% first, so you can invest this money. This is sound advice, but not always.

Let's say you have a debt with your credit card company where you pay 25% interest. Unless you find an investment that can pay you a 50% *ROI (Return On Investment)*, it will make no financial sense! It should be at least a 50% *ROI* because if the investment "only" gives you a 25% *ROI,* you will not break even, as you must later pay taxes on your capital gain.

So if you are earning a 3% interest return on your investment, but are paying 25% interest on your credit card debt, this is a net loss! If you can earn a higher return on your investment than the interest on your debt, pay yourself first and invest this money. Otherwise, pay off your balance first!

Get Rid Of Your Credit Cards, Except For One!

"Beware of little expenses; a small leak will sink a great ship."
– Benjamin Franklin

Get rid of all of your credit cards, except for one. (Keep one for business and one for personal.) Keeping a credit card is great to accumulate points for traveling and hotel stays, access airport lounges (the food is free!) and save money in foreign transaction fees when traveling overseas. In addition, credit cards, in certain countries, help you build your credit score.

Here's a Titan secret: *treat your credit card like a debit card*. Always pay your full credit card bill. The month you don't pay your credit card off, you will sabotage your financial health because this is when interest accrues. One more thing, don't fall into the trap of spending more just for the points!

Good Debt Vs. Bad Debt.

"You cannot escape the responsibility of tomorrow by evading it today."

– Abraham Lincoln

Most people don't know the difference between good debt and bad debt. Good debt is borrowing money to invest it. Bad debt is borrowing money to spend it. Good debt is taking a mortgage to buy an investment property. Bad debt is taking a mortgage to buy a house for you to live in. Good debt is borrowing money to invest in a profitable company. Bad debt is borrowing money to buy a vacation you currently cannot afford.

In summary, *good debt makes you richer, while bad debt makes you poorer.* Never go into bad debt if you can help it! And if you can't help it, get rid of bad debt as soon as possible!

Asset Vs. Liability.

*"An asset puts money in my pocket. A liability
takes money out of my pocket."*

– Robert T. Kiyosaki

The house you own but live in is not an asset, but a liability. Why? Because you must pay the mortgage, property taxes, insurance, utility bills. The house you own, but rent out to tenants, is an asset because it puts money in your pocket. Your tenants pay the mortgage, property taxes, insurance, utility bills and, ideally, you even make a bit of money as well!

If, nevertheless, you are still interested in buying a home for you to live in, here are some Titan tips:

- Only buy a house **if you can pay with cash.**
- If the above is not an option, only buy a house if you can **put down 20% of the purchase price.** If you have $20,000 for a down-payment, you can only afford a $100,000 house. The bigger your initial down-payment, the lower your monthly mortgage payments will be. It may even result in a lower interest rate as well. As the smaller the loan, the less risky for lenders, the less interest rate they will charge you!
- Stick with a **fixed mortgage payment** (including taxes and insurance) that's **under 30 percent** of your take-home income (after taxes.)

As Warren Buffet said, *"Instead of buying dream homes, the goal should be to buy a home you can afford."*

Simplify Your Lifestyle.

"Some of those who grow rich will be prudent, live within
bounds, and preserve what they have gained for their posterity.
Others, fond of showing their wealth, will be extravagant and
ruin themselves."
— Benjamin Franklin

Titans are frugal. They live quite simple lifestyles. Warren
Buffett has lived in his relatively modest home for the past
60 years. Carlos Slim purchases most of his clothing off the
rack from one of the many retail franchises he owns. And
Amancio Ortega still lives in a small apartment in La
Coruna, Spain.

Here are some Titan tips to simplify your lifestyle:

- **Have a smaller** house or apartment.
- **Move to another city or country where your**
  money stretches more. There is beauty in earning in
  dollars or euros and living in pesos or bahts.
- **Adapt a minimalist wardrobe.** As Benjamin
  Franklin said, *"When you incline to have new*
  clothes, look first well over the old ones, and see if
  you cannot shift with them another year, either by
  scouring, mending, or even patching if necessary.
  Remember, a patch on your coat, and money in your
  pocket, is better and more creditable, than a writ on
  your back, and no money to take it off."
- **Have one car.** If the total annual cost of your car,
  including installments, gas, insurance, service and
  registration, is over 10% of your income, you are
  overspending.
- **Own a second-hand car.** It will be cheaper to buy
  and the insurance cost won't be as high. Look for a
  vehicle about 3 years old and with fewer than 30,000
  miles on the clock.

- **Use the public library** instead of buying books.
- **Build a home gym** instead of spending money on a gym membership.
- **Stay healthy!** In countries with no universal health care, this will save you from costly medical bills.
- **Carpool when possible**, or better yet, work from home.
- **Sell things** in your house you don't use anymore.

There is a reason the biggest plumber in your home town has a net worth many times that of lawyers and doctors. Lawyers and doctors are pressured to buy status symbols to convince their clients and patients they are successful. Not the plumber! He can live a simpler lifestyle and put more money into his Titan investments. Over decades, the result is millions in additional wealth for the guy who unclogged toilets!

Invest In Inflation-Protected Vehicles.

"Americans are getting stronger. Twenty years ago, it took two people to carry ten dollars' worth of groceries. Today, a five-year-old can do it."

– Benjamin Graham

Inflation is a fact of life, especially since the U.S. abandoned the gold standard in 1971. In simple terms, prior to 1971, the U.S. dollars were backed by the amount of gold held in the U.S. Federal Reserve. After 1971, the U.S. government can print as much money as they find necessary. The more money that circulates, the less its value. This is why there will always be inflation, meaning there will always be consistent price increases!

To avoid the hit of inflation, you must invest in inflation-protected vehicles such as stocks, bonds and real estate income. This is why the worst investment you can have is cash! As Warren Buffett said, *"Everybody is talking about cash being king and all that sort of thing. Cash is going to become worth less over time. But good businesses are going to become worth more over time."*

This not to say that having an emergency cash fund is a bad thing, but having piles of cash just sitting around in your bank account or under your mattress is a terrible investment!

Make Your Money Work For You!

"If you want to become really wealthy, you must have your money work for you."

– John Templeton

Are you working for your money or is your money working for you?

While most people work for money, *Titans make their money work for them.* This is why you must put your money to work. You must invest your money!

You invest money only after you have saved at least 6 months of living expenses. This way, you don't risk having to sell off your stock in a rush if you get into financial difficulties.

The more your money works, the less you will have to work. Example: earning a 10 percent return on $10,000 will only net you $1,000 before taxes. But the same return on a $1,000,000 portfolio is $100,000, which has far more utility despite requiring the same effort and research.

Focus on your primary business until your investments pay off. You work hard for money, and then you let money work hard for you!

Investing Your Money.

"If you are born poor it's not your mistake,
but if you die poor it's your mistake."

– *Bill Gates*

While every Titan investor will give you a different answer about where to put your money, one thing that all Titans agree on is that "investing" your money in a savings account will not make you rich! While safe, your gains will be minimal, given the extremely low-interest rates.

A savings account is a reliable place for an emergency fund or while you are saving money for an upcoming investment. At least, it will give you an interest rate between 2% and 5%, depending on where you put your money. Once you have your emergency fund (six months of expenses), you now open another savings account for an upcoming investment. As soon as you save $10,000, invest it!

So, where should you invest your money? The short answer is in *company stock*. Either you build your own company or you buy some company stock. *But you have to become a full or partial owner of a business.* Company stocks can have relatively high returns, and if done correctly, you will be increasing your wealth before you know it!

Here are the questions Warren Buffet asks himself before making an investment in a company:

1. Do you understand the business?
2. Does the company have long-term potential?
3. Do you trust the management?
4. Is the price right?

Invest In What You Understand.

"Invest in what you know."

– Peter Lynch

Invest in what you know, understand or are passionate about. And if you know little about a certain type of investment, learn as much as you can before you invest any money in it. You want to learn as much about war before you go into one. So get yourself financially educated!

If you don't want to put in the time to understand a particular investment, your safest bet is to invest in low-risk funds like *index funds*, which track overall performance of an index like the S&P 500. This accomplishes diversification across assets and time, two very important things. Choose a low-cost index fund (Most have many "hidden fees"!). Index funds will likely outperform actively managed funds in the long term. This is why if you will invest in index funds, you should do so for at least five years.

Warren Buffett said, *"My advice to the trustee could not be more simple: Put 10% of the cash in short-term government bonds and 90% in a very low-cost S&P 500 index fund. I suggest Vanguard's. I believe the trust's long-term results from this policy will be superior to those attained by most investors – whether pension funds, institutions or individuals – who employ high-fee managers."*

If you will invest in more volatile investments or investments you particularly don't understand well, invest no more than 10% of your income, but pretend you already lost your money! As Benjamin Graham said, *"The individual investor should act consistently as an investor and not as a speculator."*

Understanding Compound Interest.

"Compound interest is the 8th wonder of the world. He who understands it, earns it; he who doesn't, pays it."
– Albert Einstein

Compound interest is when the interest, dividends, and capital gains your money has earned generate their own interest, dividends, and capital gains, and on and on in a virtuous cycle. This is how $10,000 can grow to $2,890,000 over 50 years at 12 percent!

Having Titan Finances is a slow process that takes time. You do small things every day, such as cut your expenses, generate extra income and invest your money. With time, it amounts to something. This is why Titans such as Warren Buffett always invest for the long term. As he said, *"Our favorite holding period is forever."* Avoid making an investment you can't hold for at least 10 years.

Crisis = Opportunity.

"The time to buy is when there's blood in the streets."
– Nathan Rothschild

Many Titan investors made their fortunes in times of crisis.

Warren Buffet said, *"Be fearful when others are greedy. Be greedy when others are fearful."*

And John Templeton said, *"To buy when others are despondently selling and to sell when others are greedily buying requires the greatest fortitude, even while offering the greatest reward."* A crisis often allows you to buy a dollar's worth of assets for a dime or less. Take advantage of the market when it is in a panic. Buy! When more normalized conditions return, sell! You will be left with some sizable gains. And if you can repeat this in subsequent downturns, you will end up with Titan Finances! What are the next countries that will be most affected by the next economic crisis? Invest in these countries. *Another important key factor is timing.* Knowing when to invest or buy is as important as knowing when to divest or sell. Buy those things that people are trying to get out of!

Other Titan Tips For Investing.

- **Avoid investing in what's popular.** George Soros said, *"Markets are constantly in a state of uncertainty and flux and money is made by discounting the obvious and betting on the unexpected."*
- **Invest in companies with long-term potential.** Warren Buffett said, *"If investors buy good companies, they're going to do fine 10, 20, 30 years from now."*
- **Look for bargains!** A bargain is something whose market value is lowest in relation to value. Buy companies whose value is temporarily "depressed." Therefore, Titan investing comes down to: *buying when it is the most depressed, selling when it becomes popular, and then buying the next depressed.* You sell when you find a much better bargain.

Educate Yourself Financially.

"Old men are always advising young men to save money. That's bad advice. Don't save every nickel. Invest in yourself."
— Henry Ford

Invest in your financial education. Otherwise, you will never enjoy Titan Finances, no matter how much money you make. You could make tons of money, but if you don't know how to manage your money, your expenses will always rise in direct proportion to your income. This is why no matter how much money you have, you must learn how to manage it.

As the proverb says, *"You have to learn to manage small things before you can manage bigger things."* And the same can be applied to money. When you show life you can manage your money, whether it is $100 or $100,000, life will give you more money to manage. If you learn to manage your money, you'll have plenty of it!

What matters is the person you must become to have Titan Finances. This is why most lottery winners lose all of their money soon. Because they might suddenly have millions of dollars, but they are the same person with the same thoughts and habits. *They haven't gone through the journey required to help them hold on to that money.* Go through the journey of building Titan Finances! Educate yourself. Study the habits of Titan investors. As Benjamin Franklin said, *"An investment in knowledge pays the best interest."*

Other Tips For Developing Titan Finances.

- **Have a weekly financial day** where you check your finances, savings and investments.

- **Read financial news.** Here are some Titan options: *The Economist, Wall Street Journal, Financial Times & New York Times.*
- **Automate** your savings.
- **Automate** your payments.
- Have **health insurance** (especially applies to countries with no universal health care). Otherwise, it could cause you great financial stress!
- Have **disability insurance.** What if you were to be physically impaired and, suddenly, you couldn't work?
- Have **life insurance.** What would happen to your family if something happened to you? Choose a life-term policy for 30 years to cover the worst possible outcome. Once you hit retirement age and your kids are all grown up, it doesn't make sense to continue paying for it.
- Have **auto and home insurance.** All Titans are over-insured!
- Have a **retirement plan**.

T

TITAN LEGACY

*"It's not the epitaph on your tombstone, but the record of your
deeds that may perpetuate your name after death."*

– Napoleon Hill

A Titan Legacy transcends the boundaries of time. The
words we speak and the deeds we do form the legacy we
leave behind. With or without our knowledge, day after day,
we create memories in the lives of others: our children,
grandchildren, neighbors, friends, coworkers, community.
*Like an echo, your Titan Legacy will continue resonating
once you are gone.*

Reflect on your Titan Legacy more often. Sure, it's
important to stay focused on your daily goals and To-Dos,
but occasionally, pull back from the noise – like Bill Gates
does during his "thinking weeks", and *reflect on how you
want to be remembered when you're no longer here.*

Make your mission to live your life in such a way it
touches other people's lives! Like an old Cherokee proverb
says, *"When you were born, you cried while the world
rejoiced. Live your life in such a way that when you die, the
world cries while you rejoice."*

Become Immortal.

*"To laugh often and love much; to win the respect of intelligent
persons and the affection of children; to earn the approbation
of honest citizens and endure the betrayal of false friends; to
appreciate beauty; to find the best in others; to give one's self;
to leave the world a bit better, whether by a healthy child, a
garden patch or a redeemed social condition; to have played
and laughed with enthusiasm and sung with exultation; to know
even one life has breathed easier because you have lived – this
is to have succeeded."*

– Ralph Waldo Emerson

Whether we will live forever in the future or not, it is a better, more reasonable and less selfish kind of immortality to live lives that mattered.

The easiest way to become "immortal" is to live your Titan Life, so fifty years after you die, you will be remembered by the footprints you left behind and by the lives you touched.

The goal is not to live forever, but to create something that will. To live on in the minds and hearts of generations to come is to cheat death. To live your Titan Life is to reach immortality. To make a Titan difference in the lives of others by becoming a Titan spouse, a Titan parent, a Titan friend and a Titan of your field is to live forever!

Your Titan Life is your shot at immortality. In this sense, we can say that Abraham Lincoln, Gandhi, Mother Teresa, Martin Luther King Jr., Steve Jobs, our parents, our siblings, our neighbors are still living among us.

Make A Titan Difference.

*"We're here to put a dent in the universe.
Otherwise why else even be here?*

– Steve Jobs

Your Titan Legacy is the mark you leave in those whose lives you touch. *With your mark, you can help make the world a better place.*

Measure your life not just by your net-worth, but by how many lives you are touching. Whether in your personal or professional lives, always make a Titan Difference.

A Titan difference does not lie in the big acts, but in the small actions you perform every day. For instance, if you borrow someone's car, don't bring it back gas-emptied. In fact, don't bring it back with the gas tank where it was. Bring the car back with a full tank, and washed!

Today you have a tremendous opportunity to leave things better than you found them. It might be to raise a child in such a way that he becomes a Titan; it might be a work of art; it might be a book; it might be a business; it might be a foundation; or it might be simply saying to your loved ones, *"I'm sorry I didn't say it to you more often, but I love you."*

Use your life to make the world better! The byproduct of this is *life will inevitably reciprocate you.* As they say, *"What goes around comes around!"*

Your Titan Uniqueness.

"Lives of great people remind us we can make our lives sublime and, departing, leave behind footprints in the sand of time."
– Henry Wadsworth Longfellow

While looking at the lives and legacies of Titans such as Mahatma Gandhi, Nelson Mandela, Mother Teresa, Martin Luther King Jr., Steve Jobs, we are reminded of what we humans can achieve. But we must not try to compare ourselves to them!

If you compare yourself to others, especially Titans who have been a Titan for years, you will meet disappointment. This is especially true with younger generations. They compare their results with those of "seasoned" Titans, such as Richard Branson, Roger Federer, Cristiano Ronaldo. *The most important gift you can give to others is your unique self.* In words of Ralph Waldo Emerson, *"The greatest gift is a portion of thyself."* Your uniqueness is what makes you different. Your Titan Legacy is *your* footprint in the sand of time!

Don't wait to make a difference until you get to a "position of power." If you want to change the world, start from where you are! Like Gandhi said, *"Be the change that you wish to see in the world."*

How do you want to be remembered? How does your unique "self" contribute to making the world a better place? What footprint will you leave in the sand of time? By asking yourself these questions, you will plant the seed for living a life that matters!

Have A Service Mentality.

"If you want happiness for an hour, take a nap. If you want happiness for a day, go fishing. If you want happiness for a year, inherit a fortune. If you want happiness for a lifetime, help somebody."

– *Chinese proverb*

For centuries, Titans have suggested the same thing: *Happiness is found in helping others.* Titans love being Titans, not for the sake of power, but for the meaningful and purposeful impact they can create. *Being a Titan and living a Titan life is about serving others.*

Whether Gandhi, Mandela, Mother Teresa, Martin Luther King Jr., they all agreed that *the real purpose of life is to serve, to be of use, to uplift those around us and to be helpful.* Albert Einstein said, *"Try not to become a man of success – but rather a man of value."*

Leo Tolstoy said, *"The sole meaning of life is to serve humanity."*

And Friedrich Nietzsche said, *"Whatever you do, always serve others. How could I serve more people today? The rest is pursuing a selfish goal and this will always make you unhappy. The whole purpose of life is, in my opinion, to use your potential circumstances to show your potential to serve the world."*

Have a service mentality! Most people refuse to serve others because they feel like they are lowering themselves to them – this is why customer service is so poor in many countries. On the other hand, Titans know that serving others is a sign of greatness.

So, if you want to live a happy life, ask yourself, *"How can I serve the most people?"*

Giving Is Receiving.

"For it is in giving that we receive."
– Francis of Assisi

Most people are takers. Titans are givers. While most people live in a world of mental scarcity, Titans find joy in giving. They know that the "richest" persons are those who give the most!

Many people say, *"If I had millions, I would be a giver as well."* This is an excuse! *Giving is an attitude, no matter how much money you have.* John Templeton started giving away before he became a billionaire. As we said before, money will only magnify who you are!

Help those in need. Donate anonymously. Make someone smile. Go through life giving and touching other people's lives. This is how you live a Titan Life! As Winston Churchill said, *"We make a living by what we get; we make a life by what we give."*

And one more thing, if life has something Titan coming to you, take it! *In the same way that Titans are givers, they also know how to receive gifts from the universe.* So stop saying, *"I can't accept it."* Instead, say, *"Thank you!"*

Other Titan Tips For Giving.

- Go to a nice restaurant and order a bottle of the best wine. Have a glass and **leave the rest of the wine for the kitchen staff.**
- **Buy coffee for the person standing behind you** in line.
- **Say hello to strangers** with a big smile on your face!
- **Give your undivided attention** when you are talking to someone.

Inspire Others.

"The greatest good you can do for another is not just to share your riches, but to reveal to him his own."
– Benjamin Disraeli

Besides material possessions and money, there's so much you can give others. *People need inspiration!*

We're living in the most amazing time in human history – and yet, every day, we see people who don't know it and don't feel it!

Titans, through their deeds, inspire others to become Titan themselves. By respecting, listening to, and encouraging others, Titans make others feel "Titan." As Ayn Rand said, *"The sight of an achievement is the greatest gift that a human being can offer others."*

Use the remaining of your days to uplift, encourage and inspire others. Make the world better because you were here! As you live your Titan Life, you will inspire others to do the same. The result, a better world for all of us!

Titan Family Legacy.

"Most people think they need to make a better world for their children, but the reality is we need to make better children for our world."

– Carlos Slim

The best legacy you can leave your children is not money, but the memories, the teachings, the bonding, the love. It's not what you leave to your children, but what you leave *in* them!

Create Titan moments with your children and build Titan relationships with them. Instill in them Titan values such as honesty, kindness, character, respect, empathy. Don't teach them about love, but make them *experience love!* And most importantly, show them the possibility by living your own Titan Life, so they will be inspired to also live their own Titan Lives!

Other Tips For Leaving A Titan Family Legacy.

- **Leave a library** as a legacy to your children.
- **Write a journal** documenting your children's lives' most important events or victories. Give it to them the day they marry or have a child.
- **Put their interests** above your own.

Titan Skill Legacy.

"If you would not be forgotten as soon as you are dead, either write something worth reading or do something worth writing about."

– Benjamin Franklin

Your mission in life is to share your gifts and value with as many people as possible.

Don't do it for the money. Do it because you want to change the world! Don't worry about success. *Focus on your Titan Skill and on bringing value and helping as many people as you can.* Create a product that will improve people's lives for generations!

When Steve Jobs was starting Apple, he had a Titan Vision, and he shared his vision with the then Head of Pepsi, John Sculley. Steve told John, *"Do you really want to sell sugar water for the rest of your life, or do you want to come with me and change the world?"* And Steve changed the world! And the world, today, is a better place because Steve was in it.

The more people you help, the more value you bring with your product or service, the "richer" you will become mentally, emotionally, spiritually, and, yes, financially.

Titan Community Legacy.

*"The one who plants trees, knowing that he will never sit in
their shade, has at least started to understand
the meaning of life."*

– Rabindranath Tagore

When former Prime Minister of Pakistan, Nawaz Sharif, was asked about Mother Teresa, he said, *"She was a rare and unique individual who lived long for higher purposes. She was one of the highest examples of service to our humanity."*
Titans throughout history have been all about improving the community. Confucius said, *"Pursuing one's own self-interest is not necessarily bad, but enhancing the greater good is better and more righteous."*

Find a way to serve the community, whether it is your neighborhood, your town, your state, your country or the world, and your life will be transformed!

See your life as a drop in an ever-flowing river and be glad to contribute your part to the great stream of life.

Other Tips For Leaving A Titan Community Legacy.

- **Get out of your house and find those who live in worse conditions**. Meet them, talk to them, understand them. Live among them. Be one of them. And see how you could contribute to making their lives better.

- **Volunteer.** Help at homeless centers. Help the sick, those with disabilities, those who are dying.

- **Each time you meet someone, treat them as if it were the last time you will see them**, because it may well be the last time you see them. And when you treat someone as though it were going to be the last time you saw them, you will make them feel special.

And when you make someone feel special, you become a Titan who will be remembered by the way you made them feel, even when you are not around anymore. They will not remember your possessions, but they will remember *how you made them feel*!

Titan Environmental Legacy.

"Treat the earth well. It was not given to you by your parents, it was loaned to you by your children. We do not inherit the Earth from our ancestors, we borrow it from our children."
– Native American proverb

We cannot define our Titan Legacies without considering our impact on the planet as well. *Being a Titan means nothing if you don't care about the environment.*

By 2050, scientists predict there will be more plastic than fish in the world's oceans. Meanwhile, clueless politicians deny the damage we are causing to the environment.

The planet needs your help too! Remember, we don't own the planet, *we are just curating it for future generations.*

While you reflect on the legacy you want to leave behind, consider how also to reduce your negative impact on the planet. Here are some small behaviors that can create a Titan impact:

- **Follow the three "R's"** (Reduce, Reuse and Recycle) to conserve natural resources and landfill space.
- **Conserve water.** The less water you use, the less runoff and wastewater will eventually end up in the ocean.
- Choose **sustainable seafood** choices.
- Bring a **reusable shopping bag.**

- **Use LED light bulbs.** They reduce greenhouse gas emissions.
- **Turn off the lights** when you leave the room.
- **Plant trees.** They provide food and oxygen and help combat climate change.
- **Use green cleaning products** around the house and office.
- **Bike more.** Drive less.
- **Educate yourself,** so you can help others understand the importance of taking care of our environment.

Titan Generation.

"I fear the day that technology will surpass our human interaction. The world will have a generation of idiots."
– Albert Einstein

Until the late '60s, courses in civic studies were common in schools around the world, and they often focused on teaching students values and manners.

In 2011, all federal funding for civic and social studies in the U.S. was eliminated. Ever since, other countries have followed the same trend. Schools are also losing their music, arts and gym classes.

In order to "compete" in this global economy, educational systems around the world are prioritizing mathematics, science and reading.

And I wonder, what type of legacy are we leaving for the future generations? What happened to manners and human values, such as generosity, respect, compassion, empathy, justice, creativity, grit and self-control? If governments around the world believe that teaching values to children is their parents' job, what happens to the children of adults who never learned these values themselves?

When people are becoming more and more selfish and unaware of other people's needs, governments should bring subjects such as civic and social studies, music, art and gym back to their educational systems. *Our future Titan generations need these as much as they need mathematics and science.*

Our Titan Humanity.

"We are caught in an inescapable network of mutuality, tied in a single garment of destiny. Whatever affects one directly, affects all indirectly."
— Martin Luther King, Jr.

As I am finishing writing this book, the new Coronavirus is racing around the world. While recognizing the impact of this now-confirmed pandemic in the world, I believe that the Coronavirus has come to teach us, the world, a lesson: *we, the human family, are interdependent.* We are all in the same boat! When a country sneezes, the whole world catches a cold. No country in the world, no matter how "powerful" they think they are, can survive alone. This is why, instead of being arrogant and selfish, *it's time for all the countries to work together in a spirit of cooperation.*

Often, we focus on our "differences," whether it is skin color, language, religion, culture, instead of focusing on the huge bond we all share: *our humanness.* These perceived differences are part of the problem!

Germany and France were enemies for many years; now, they are allies. Women could not vote; now they can vote, at least in most democratic countries. People of the same sex could not get married, now, gay marriage is legal in most of the developed world. All it takes is *a change of perception.* And the only way we can change our perceptions is through *education.*

It's time we realize that to survive in this global world in which we live, *we must all come together.* The point of globalization is not to be free to travel to other countries or enjoy certain products from other countries, but to see our humanness in others. *We must subordinate our individual interests and selfishness to the broader interests of the human race as a whole.*

The Coronavirus is a wake-up call for the seven billion members of this Titan human family! It has pointed out at what we, as humans, are still missing: *human cooperation.* Aristotle once said, *"A man doesn't become a hero until he can see the root of his own downfall."* The Coronavirus has pointed out how we could all fall unless we come together and cooperate as humans.

Contrary to those "leaders" who profit from war, making us believe in the concept of "we vs. they," the Coronavirus has made us realize that the entire world is part of "we." And for this, alone, we should thank the Coronavirus.

I am convinced that we will come together to eradicate the Coronavirus and will all come out stronger and more united. *It's time we realize our oneness as human beings!*

FINAL WORDS.

Be Content, But Never Satisfied.

"I have walked that long road to freedom. I have tried not to falter; I have made missteps along the way. But I have discovered the secret that after climbing a great hill, one only finds that there are many more hills to climb. I have taken a moment here to rest, to steal a view of the glorious vista that surrounds me, to look back on the distance I have come. But I can only rest for a moment, for with freedom come responsibilities, and I dare not linger, for my long walk is not ended."

– Nelson Mandela

Contentment is something we should all strive for. To be content is to be happy in the life you're living; to have the ability to be grateful for the blessings you have and enjoy every moment of your life.

But to say that you're satisfied with everything in your life is just a way to settle for mediocrity, to give up on your dreams. If you ever feel "completely satisfied" with everything in your life, it means you haven't set the bar high enough. It means you have settled for being good rather than striving to be a Titan.

Life is like climbing a dune. Sometimes you climb and make no progress, but the second you stop climbing, you start descending without noticing. The second you stop learning and growing in every aspect of life, you start to die.

Never stop climbing! Never allow yourself to be completely satisfied with your life! The only time you should allow yourself to stop striving to be better is when you're six feet under. As Richard Bach said, *"How will I know when I've completed my mission? If you are still breathing, you are not done."*

Ruben Lhasa, March 16th, 2020.

ACKNOWLEDGEMENTS.

First and foremost, thank you to my Titan wife, Romina, for your unconditional love and for always believing in me.

To our sons, Adolfo, Nicolas and Kenzo for inspiring me to be the best version of myself.

To my parents, for all the sacrifices you made, so I could create my Titan Life.

To Deogracias Medina Delgado for teaching me humility, respect and self-discipline through karate.

To Rodolfo Alvarez Gonzalez for being a Titan friend.

To Mehrdad O. Koupai for trusting me enough to sponsor my U.S. visa when I first moved to Los Angeles.

To Ruben Aghai, Noel Howard, Phil Barlow, Sandy Stewart, Greg Burkart and Rafael Angelo, Anthony Pontrello, Arthur Mendoza, Wendy Urquhart, Chris and Jamie McGurk, Peter and Kathy Adee and Alan Kaye for opening the doors to your homes, and also your hearts.

To Paulo Coelho for making me love reading through his masterpiece *The Alchemist.*

To those Titans who inspired me – and continue to inspire me with your "Titanness."

To those who didn't believe in me, thanks for the "extra fuel!"

And finally, to the thousands of people whom I have met through my trips around the world, thank you for opening my mind, making my life richer and bettering me as a human!

Made in the USA
Monee, IL
30 October 2020